Praise

for *Junkyard Princess*

"*Junkyard Princess* is a generous, wise, and deeply moving memoir. Robyn Saunders Wilson has gifted us a beautifully written and powerful exploration of inherited trauma and the enduring love that seeks to heal. Don't miss this one!"

—Alan Drew, author of *Gardens of Water* and *The Recruit*

"*Junkyard Princess* is a collection of vignettes that drive down vulnerable and youthful roads unexpected, yet familiar. Aching with nostalgia, Saunders claims "we are children without breaks", but through scraps of memories and heaps of time, the breaks of reality fast approach. Through these raw recollections—some shiny, some rusted, some sexy red and some painfully dented, the reader is led by Saunders to the beauty and richness of myth in truth amidst self-discovery."

—SarahAnn Harvey, Founding Editor of *Pile Press*

"A love story if ever there was one. Humming with grit and humor, like the Plymouth Fury III. *Junkyard Princess* hums with windows-down honesty, cruisin'-speed wit, and a fresh grease marker. You won't be able to put it down!"

—Jessica Amos, TEDx Speaker and founder of Stay With Yourself

"I laughed. I cried. *Junkyard Princess* gave me all the feels… a tender slice of life filled with humor, heartbreak, and unexpected moments of meaning. Just when you think you know where her story is headed, a surprise turn invites you deeper—opening memories, sparking connection, and reminding you how beautifully human we all are. This touching, relatable story will make you laugh, smile, and stay with you long after the final page."

—Carlee Wright, Editor, *Press Play Magazine*

JUNKYARD
PRINCESS

A memoirella

BY
Robyn Saunders Wilson

Copyright © 2026 by Robyn Saunders Wilson

Banana Pitch Press supports copyright.
Copyright supports artists and promotes free speech.
Thank you for buying an authorized version of this book
and for not unlawfully copying and distributing this text,
which hurts our authors and our press.

An earlier version of "It's On" appeared in *Pile Press*.

Library of Congress
Paperback ISBN: 979-8-9913071-4-7
Ebook ISBN: 979-8-9913071-6-1

This Book's Team:
Production and Managing Editor: Michelle Kicherer
Editorial Intern: Luka Cohn
Book design: Gwendolyn Schulte at GRS Editorial, LLC
Cover art: Ryan Floyd Johnson

Banana Pitch Press
bananapitch.com

For Harry

JUNKYARD PRINCESS

Chapter 1

Amber and Rose Stained Glass

My mom motioned us into the living room for what looked to be a serious discussion. I didn't remember doing anything too bad during the day, but as I checked my little brother's face for potential offense or guilt, I wondered if this was a trap for a run-in with the wooden spoon. My mom was looking at my dad and let her gaze rest there. Something was up—she usually didn't make eye contact with Dad.

Dad removed his glasses. The lenses were hefty, lightly coated with grease. His vision was so poor he rarely realized how dirty they were. He stabbed his eye with a thick finger in an attempt to remove the debris caught in the corner. His thin lips were slightly swollen, his face stubborn; he knew we were going to resist him about the subject of our meeting.

"I've decided to—" He stopped himself, glanced at Mom for the go-ahead and what I'd learn was feigned partnership. Mom didn't give away much with her expression, just kept staring forward, unsmiling. "We've decided to buy a wrecking yard," Dad finished.

A what?

A wrecking yard? A junk yard? A big yard lined with rusty old cars and broken machinery and car parts and murderous dogs and who knows what else? Who decides to buy a wrecking yard? What kind of purchase is that? You can buy a car, a house, new shoes, but a wrecking yard? I looked over at my brother with those thoughts racing through my head but Ryan was only five and not very interested. After another beat he left the room to play with his truck. But I was nine: old enough, unfortunately, to be left all alone with those people. My dad was giddy and I could tell my mom was putting on a good show, trying to look brave. The details continued. "It's a reputable auto wrecking yard. We'll sell car parts and antique cars. I've always wanted to own my own wrecking yard."

Huh. A wrecking yard.

As career pursuits go, "junkyard owner" was not on my radar. I knew of the usual. Doctors, dentists, lawyers, teachers, scientists, and artists. Tried and true endeavors. Who did Harry Saunders think he was creating a new vocation category? But it turns out, the idea had been on his mind for years and we were just getting the memo. He had dreamed of it since he was a little boy growing up in the San Fernando Valley. Son of a mechanic and an absentee mother, he never excelled in school and was too scrawny and awkward for sports. There was no one around to tell him that reading and writing might be important or to realize that something was getting in the way of knowing the alphabet to begin with. But it didn't matter. His education about the world came in a different form. Metal. By the time he was fourteen in 1957, he had dropped out of school and began hustling metals, learning his trade from Old Man Sam the Jew, a guy he met at the local scrap yard. What started out with recycling tin pop cans for twenty-five cents a pound soon led to learning the nuances of aluminum, iron, steel, and copper. Not only did he learn how to identify various grades, he also watched as supply and demand ebbed and flowed depending on how these materials were used around the world: building nations, aiding wars, and constructing assembly lines for all the baubles demanded for modern life. Harry Saunders may have been illiterate, but he understood the basics of economics at an early age. He scavenged the valley looking for clean materials and when he didn't find them, he would strip down car parts or other machinery to their purest level of metalhood until the material was ready for the scrap yard.

And so, Harry Saunders dreamed the biggest dream he could. He imagined having a huge yard or warehouse to store and prepare his metals for the scrap yard. It would be his way of stockpiling valuables; his Fort Knox.

I remained quiet taking it all in, suspicious of the details they were not sharing. My dad was always going out on jobs, collecting cars and metal, often using elaborate comealong straps to muscle them into his big truck and bring them back to his tiny piece of land in Laguna Beach.

If he had outgrown the confines of his little rented plot, that seemed weird, but maybe not unreasonable. I shifted my weight, feeling that something more was coming.

"So we'll be moving as soon as we can sell our house."

There it was. A firebomb landed in my stomach, scorching its way through every cell in my body. The heat from the fear painted me red. To where? To where? Where are we going?

"The wrecking yard is in a place called Hesperia, about two hours from here," he explained. My mom remained pale and silent. Moving? To a place that's not Orange County? That couldn't possibly be safe. Helter Skelter, the Night Stalker, and other villains populated the land outside the walled fortress of our organized community—we had been told this by all the adults since we were old enough to get abducted, murdered, or harvested for our organs. It just wasn't safe to be out there… beyond.

I ran to my room, careful to close my door without the dramatic slam the situation actually warranted. I was trying to avoid pushing my dad's anger button. He hated closed doors. Already angry or not, I could count on him to kick my door open with his steel-toed boots. It wasn't truly an act of malice; more a side effect of his deep-seated awkwardness and fear of what might be happening on the other side. It's like his brain was incapable of turning off before his hand turned the knob and his foot made contact at the bottom of the door. The insertion point on my door was permanent and we no longer attempted to patch the hole. But that day I needed sanctuary for my fears that quickly gave way to tears.

In that pre-Google era, there wasn't a quick reference tool to figure out where the new place was. The "H" encyclopedia was not helpful either. No entries found.

Hesperia. Sounded exotic. I tucked myself into the corner of my canopied bed and began imagining. I pictured it: a white three-story Victorian house with stained glass windows casting rose and amber light onto dark wood floors and secret panels leading to passages that only I would know about; a white picket fence surrounding perfected green lawns and multiple gardens; an ancient oak tree shading the front porch with limbs low enough to climb. Sidewalks lining the streets, me out there riding my bike with all my new friends. It was so beautiful I could hardly breathe. Colleen would be so jealous. This was a hundred times better than her new lavender room at her mom's house.

Then there was a gentle knock on the door, without the usual accompanying kick. "Rob, let's go for a ride so I can show you."

I closed my eyes, holding fast to the image of my new Disney-approved home. What was that? Was that a tingle I felt? Was I feeling excited? I punched down the fear and let excitement take over, making my way out of the canopied sanctuary, opening the door to my new hope.

My brother and I loaded up into the back seat of the old 1973 Chevelle station wagon. My mom sat in the front passenger seat, where she remained silent for the entirety of our ride, which turned out to be much longer than I was expecting. Ryan was fussy as usual, squirming around on the pleather seat, tossing his seatbelt away from his scrawny body. Sometimes we were friendly but oftentimes he was a pain in the ass. Eventually the tedium of not knowing *how much further 'til we get there?* got the best of him and he passed out, sweat matting his white-blonde hair, his skin stuck to the pleather. Out the window, the sky started losing its coastal blue tint and the houses were becoming misshapen without the uniformity of tract housing rules. Green turned to brown. Sterile white sidewalks transformed to dusty footpaths. The radio turned to static, out of reach of big city reception. My mom finally reached across the bench seat, swatting the knob to Off.

Before that time, most of our road trips had been to Hollywood, where my great-grandmother lived. That journey allowed us to traverse the patchwork of disparate cities, houses, and people until we reached our destination in the glamorous Los Feliz neighborhood, with its Spanish tiled mansions, mysterious courtyards, and movie stars. That evening's journey was taking us to someplace completely different—houses began to disappear altogether and any shred of natural life seemed to be swallowed by dry earth. After nearly two hours of silence, my dad barked into the backseat.

"This is called the Cajon Pass."

I startled, looking out the window. The highway lurched upward, steep. A stark, treeless mountain on one side, vast views to nothing or possibly hell on the other;

the San Andreas fault loomed below, waiting to break the earth apart at a whim. Sunburnt land and dry bushes for as far as the eye could see. Finally, we summited. A clear separation between who we were and who we were going to be, no three-story Victorian house in sight.

I closed my eyes, willing away the ache growing in my belly. The car slowed, exiting the highway. I no longer felt the sun on my face; the warmth was blocked by low-hanging clouds and rain needles hitting the windshield. No one was talking and my eyes remained shut until the pungency of my brother's moist security blanket was all I could smell wafting through the car. Maybe the blanket was attempting to soothe me as it did Ryan, but that thing was oozing with a spoiled-milk germiness.

The car stopped.

Nobody moved. Not even Ryan as he came to from his sweaty nap. All eyes peered at the empire before us—a locked fortress of steel fencing as far as the eye could see.

There may have been words shared. If there were, I did not hear them. Later we would use our own keys to walk through the official entrance, assemble yard hands, order business cards, sweep floors, fill the gumball machine, and steal its quarters. In the weeks to come, we would light the wood stove for heat, run in and out of the many doors before the wind could slam them shut on our lanky limbs, and climb up and down the many shelves hiding from the adults in the high, dark landings. In the years to come, we would scramble across the sandy acres of cars on foot or forklift. But in that moment, we were frozen, on the outside unable to look in—our future on hold. There was still time to say no and yet no words came from my mom. Worse yet, my own words of protest were on lockdown. Where did my voice go? I closed my eyes again, pulling my pink windbreaker tight around me and unbuckling then re-buckling my seatbelt for safety.

Though I was sick with fear, I also knew it was time to be brave. And I knew how to do that. I had negotiated my life before. I'd learned lessons I wish I didn't have to learn, among those: how to be brave. Another: how not to complain. So young, I already knew how to be older than my years to protect myself. I stuck my hand out the window, tested the air. I was ready.

Chapter 2
Rise of the Machine

And so the dream was realized faster than expected. My parents sold our respectable little house and we were off to Hesperia, population 35,000, a desert community on the way to Las Vegas. Home of our new wrecking yard.

"I never thought he'd call my bluff," my mom revealed in a conversation decades later. My mom, queen of our greasy empire. Even now I can't picture it, but she had been there prodding my dad along, staring at the walls, stepping over the blobs of machinery, paying the bills. A far cry from her former life as a housewife, when she'd quietly spend her days volunteering in our classrooms, sewing, watching her soaps, and taking care of all the mom details that—let's be honest—go unnoticed until they dry up and all hell breaks loose.

"What do you mean?" I'd never heard that before. The thought of my mom having a poker face seemed unlikely.

"I knew he wanted this, but I never thought he'd make us go through with a move like *that*. I just kept agreeing, and then before I knew it, everything was sold. What could

I do then? I couldn't deny him." My mom the enabler. She could never say no.

When we were first setting up shop, my dad was beside himself with happiness, a constant inventory of his empire rumbling off his tongue: "Four acres, steel fence, two warehouses, three forklifts, one-thousand cars, and a junkyard dog." He'd repeat the list again and again as if to assure us it was indeed a treasure. We were less certain. But there it was: tall corrugated steel inching through sand and tumbleweed containing remnants of metal parts, looking for a second act before death by corrosion. Gnarled Joshua trees stretched sharp limbs for as far as the eye could see—brittle warriors warning us to run. A train track ran parallel to the fence. Every so often a freight train would whistle its way through as if taunting us with its more spectacular endpoints.

In those first few days, we left Dad to his empire and pursued a more tangible goal: a new home. We found a house to rent a few miles away in what was considered a "desirable" neighborhood for its proximity to a good elementary school. At some point I wrote a hopeful letter to my old fourth grade class, boasting of the land that would easily house seven pools and all the bike jumps we could shovel—not to mention the huge driveway for roller skating. I yearned for the manicured streets of our old life and my friends. I missed my best friend, Colleen with a profound ache that would rattle through me in sobs during the night.

Luckily, my new fourth grade teacher, Mr. Wells, understood how rudderless I was and gently nudged me toward purpose. "Robyn, I need your help. Could you organize a library for us?" He spoke my language. At my old school the library was one of the best parts of the day. (This would become a constant refrain and did not win me any friends. *At my old school* we had gymnastics with Olympic-sized balance beams and bars; *at my old school* we learned the Dewey Decimal system in first grade in Library Science class; *at my old school* we had books that we actually read because it was the best elementary school in all of California.)

With the help of the other new kid, Stephen, we gathered books from home and dusty corners of the school, organized the library's shelves alphabetically, then created a checkout system complete with a date stamp. There was a place and a process for everything, my internal whisper a constant: "Don't deviate, Robyn, and all will be okay. Be good. Homework—do extra; cleanliness—don't let dust live; soccer—show how strong and normal you are; bike—throw yourself off the steepest hill; run—don't stop, be faster than the others; daydream—consider other planets and galaxies—maybe you're a princess from another galaxy here to take notes."

So went the internal voice I used when I needed help taming what I called my "inner monster," the shapeshifter of rage that had taken up residence in my belly. I was slowly becoming an unstoppable machine, the only way I knew to counter both the chaos of our new life and that of the adults, who I was pretty sure had lost their minds as well as my trust.

And yet, one thing we could all trust was the strange calm of our car graveyard. I spent my afternoons after school wandering the sea of broken machinery, following winding paths of sand through injured and beaten auto bodies, gingerly tip-toeing on broken glass, rubbing my fingers across dented fenders and smooth molding. There was one car in particular that I always made my way to even as the wind escalated in the afternoon, dirtying my white Nikes and thrusting my thin body into the stacked cars. It was a black, very rusty 1947 Chrysler limousine, complete with bullet holes in the windshield. Later I would become a voyeur, scavenging the cars for relics left behind by their owners—but I never violated the old Chrysler. Instead, I would lean against the car next to it, terrified that a Las Vegas gangster, whom I had christened Guido, would jump out of the rusty trunk and strangle me with a coat hanger. If I stared at the car long enough, I could see blood stains from the assassination that brought it to our graveyard.

Up and down the aisles I would go, scrambling in all directions, scaling the cars stacked two and three high, my own private climbing gym. These discarded cars of varying provenance were filled with remnants of former lives: Van Halen cassettes, report cards, food wrappers, winter coats, beer bottles, blood stains, and once, a thumb sans its hand lodged in a gear shifter. The shock value of these treasures diminished with time, but the importance of these cast-off stories settled in and took up residence, teaching me all the ways we are expendable.

Chapter 3

Aristocracy, or: Becoming a Princess

Afternoons at the junkyard slowly evolved into weekends as well. By the time I was twelve, I had a little blue uniform shirt with a white name patch embroidered in red cursive: *Robyn*. My dad had the adult version of my shirt, his name patch emblazoned: *Harry*. They didn't pass out name patches to just anyone. I wasn't a volunteer or simply a doting daughter. This was my first legitimate job. I like to think my dad enjoyed my enthusiasm and thought I'd be a great addition to the afternoon and weekend crew. Closer to the truth was that he simply needed an extra body when my mom left for the day and because she demanded Saturdays off. Regardless, I was excited to have purpose with a paycheck. Plus, my weekly earnings would help me buy the new blue bike I'd had my eye on, and maybe get to my boom box upgrade sooner rather than later.

In the spirit of now being colleagues, I liked to call my dad Harry at work. I would follow him everywhere, his legs moving in sharp scissor-like motion, always carrying him to the next customer or car or argument, hustling up and down the neatly organized rows of his empire. He'd bark out tools to me: "Nine-sixteenths open-end wrench! Three-eighths-inch drive! Half-inch swivel socket with the six-inch extension! I'm going to need a Phillips, too!" And I'd be off, jumping over tires and bulky shapes of metal until I made it to the greasy red toolbox to dig out the loot. Just as quickly, I'd rush back to his side and wait for him to assess my tool-finding ability. Speed and accuracy were important qualities. I did not want to duplicate the run through four acres of sand in the 110-degree desert sun.

I soon proved myself loyal and as a reward, my dad promoted me to counter girl, a big step up from "tool lackey." My new role meant I was in charge of greeting all customers who came in the windowless metal door, as well as answering two phone lines and a hotline that connected us to other reputable auto dismantlers throughout the land. This was big. I felt honored that my dad would trust me in that way. I didn't know if I was the right person for the job, though. My shyness often modulated the tremble of my voice and the quaking of my knees, especially in those initial days. But still, I pressed on.

～ ✕ ～

Soon, Harry had a following. I can't think of a single afternoon where his groupies weren't holding court in the office, one greasy-handed fellow on each barstool. More accurately, the clan of men who hung out everyday were probably hoping Harry would hook them up with cheap parts or at least a beer. These guys, a mismatched cabal of car enthusiasts, had other lives ranging from carpenter, mechanic, farmer, and/or drunk. Together, they joined forces to provide me with my first ever professional coaching sessions.

The guys had many, many pro-tips for me, starting with lowering my voice so I could sound more womanly (older) when customers called. I was not remotely womanly. Aside from my not womanliness—I was only twelve, you know—I was also far from cool. I had certain passions: for example, I loved fashion, new wave music, soccer, Molly Ringwald movies, and Adam Carney (a crush-worthy classmate; unrequited). But my androgynous twelve-year-old self whispered *vanilla nondescript genderless child* to the world. A freckled face framed by mousy brown hair that refused to find shape after repeated home cuttings. I presented very small despite my 5'8" frame, often shrinking into the background or simply lower because none of my friends were as tall as me.

One day I even tried to unvanilla myself by buying makeup at the local drugstore. I thought I might paint on a new look. But when I set my tubes of lipstick and mascara on the counter, the checker refused to sell it to me because she thought I was a boy. "Oh hon, boys don't wear makeup. I'll just take that back." My face stung hot and I silently moved out of the way. But I wasn't completely defeated. I mean, Molly Ringwald wouldn't give up, right? She would roll her eyes and ironically pout up a new idea—or maybe just pout and all would come. Regardless, I just needed to work a little harder, be more inventive. Safe to say that sounding womanly and sexy was not much of an option, but I channeled my inner Molly Ringwald and did my best for the cause. I lowered my voice an octave and let the words smoothly drip off my tongue: "Thank you for calling B&R. Can I help you?"

Practice. Practice. Practice.

"Th–ank you–for cal–"

"Th–ank you–for cal–ling B&R..."

"Th–ank you–for cal–ling B&R–Can I–help you?"

Think woman.

Be woman.

I sat perched at the yellow formica counter, swiped from a diner years before, waiting for phone calls and customers to come in. My stomach tightened every time the phone rang; my knees did an immediate quiver. Okay, lower voice, listen, think: what do they need, what questions do I need to remember to ask. I took notes on every call, trying my best to sell a part without sounding too terrified, while attempting to maintain my version of a confident, sexy woman who knows a thing or two about the world and is allowed to buy makeup from the local drugstore. From time to time my dad would wander through the office, gesturing at me with pride to the groupies. The groupies, proud of their coaching, would silently nod in agreement, as if to say, "Not quite junkyard princess, but on her way." All the while I was having inner freak-outs, terrified the phone would ring and I would have to start the process all over again.

To combat the fear, I started memorizing. I would walk the yard before work, eyeballing the long lines of stacked cars and trucks. Trucks, vans, and heavy equipment lined the west side of the first aisle, with the General Motors family across the way, followed by the Fords. Chryslers and Plymouths could be found on Aisles Two and Three. Any foreign cars, of which there were few, could be found on Aisle Three on the east side. At the south side of the yard, vintage cars from the 1930s through 1950s held court two deep, as we did not stack these cars for fear of damaging them further. When I wasn't physically taking stock of inventory, I read. I read every car manual, every Hollander interchange book I could get my hands on.

The Hollander books in particular were of great comfort to me, as theirs was a system similar to the library—categories for specific regions of a vehicle that then allowed me to drill down to individual parts. Every single part had a specific number. And that number, which was hand-scrawled onto the part with a fluorescent yellow grease marker, paved the road to first my identifying the correct item on our shelves, then if it wasn't there, decoding which other cars out in the yard used that exact same part. And when all that failed, I eavesdropped on the groupies and tried to pick up the lingo… Holley four barrels, Goats, Mopar Hemi's, rotors, drums, horsepower. I was a fraud. I could talk the talk like an old-timer but could not pick a 350 Chevy motor out of a line up. Most of my interactions at that point would go something like:

"Hi. What can I get for you today? Uh, huh. Okay, an automatic transmission for a seventy-six Granada. Sure, hang on for a second." Press the hold button. Grab the big dusty blue Hollander Interchange book from the shelf. Plop in lap, spreading knees slightly apart to anchor the hefty volume. Quickly flip through the soft thinning pages to the transmission tab. Skim, skim, skim. Few different ones. Okay. Column shift of floor shift? Motor size? Those were my considerations for the drill down. Got it. "Harry!" I'd call out the back door, "I need a C-four auto trans for a seventy-six Granada. What do ya got back there?" My dad would come running into the office with a nod of his head and raise two fingers. "Tell him a hundred and twenty-five, Robyn."

To that I would smile into the phone. "Yes, sir. I have a couple in stock. Uh, huh. A hundred and fifty dollars." I may have been a fraud but I knew how to make extra cash early on.

As the afternoons and Saturdays elapsed, the stomach pains went away—or at least, weren't as sharp. I was still a fraud, but time made me a better actress. And besides, the groupies and endless yard hands—the Freddies, Bobbys, Wallys, Jims, Vietnam Dans, and Clean Franks— didn't have the I.Q. to call my bluff. Nor did they want to hurt my feelings. On the outside, they were a rough-looking crew, and yet, their tone with me was gentle, never raising a voice or tossing an obscenity my way. They bumbled about, following my orders, gathering and cleaning parts for our customers who were either curious about my novelty act or thoroughly annoyed that they were at the mercy of a kid, and a girl at that. Eye contact after the initial eye-roll was rare. New customers would look over my head or shoulder, anywhere but my face, willing a grown up, preferably a man, to swing through the warehouse door and save them from my polite assistance. My dad would just run his fingers through his thick black hair and laugh it off.

※

As junkyards go, ours had the outward appearance of dignity. Or, that's what we liked to tell folks when they called. "Yep, we're at the corner of Darwin and Santa Fe, all paved streets. Bright green building. Can't miss us. Yep, park in the parking lot. It's paved, too. You'll see a sign at the entrance for the office. Come on in." And once they made it down the paved road to the corner of Darwin and Santa Fe, parked in an actual parking lot, and sauntered through the metal gate to the heavy metal door marked "Office," they would find me perched at the large yellow formica counter. In this dreary office, with its scuffed checkerboard floors and dust-caked windows, the counter presented as a ray of sunshine—a happy spectacle of normality.

That counter was a statement piece declaring, "Look, we are not dirty people." This is no junk yard. No pick n' pull. We are full service. You ask the questions. We have answers and expertise. You do not get to roam the aisles. That is for us. A pinnacle of professionalism. In fact, we belong to a professional organization of wrecking yards, of the loftily-titled *dismantling* yards, if you will, who aim to make the world a better place through our eco-friendly process of recycling. We even have lobbyists who argue on our behalf before Congress. What are lobbyists? Doesn't matter. This is a serious business.

And yet, despite all this outwardly competent decorum, we had a knowledge gap. We would never be accused of being mechanics. We did not know how to fix cars or anything else. Destruction rather than repair was our hustle.

⸺ X ⸺

I remember one day hanging out on Aisle One before we opened the doors to the public. My dad was at the helm of the big yellow forklift, navigating it toward a station wagon he needed to bring into one of the bays for disassembly. In a split second he went from serious and focused Dad, Captain of Heavy Machinery to "I have the best idea" Dad, Captain of Jolly Town, his face full of mischief. The Captain of Jolly Town was my favorite of the dads. Belly laughs and stupidity guaranteed. "Come here, Rob," he called down to my lowly perch between the greasy asphalt and the beginning of the sand row. I didn't waste any time. I knew exactly what was coming next. This was the moment I had been waiting for since being officially hired for my esteemed position. My dad expertly moved the gear shift to neutral, pulled up on the emergency brake, and clambered out of the seat, hopping to the ground below. "Up you go!" he shouted.

I pulled myself up into the rig and slid into the seat. So tall. My forks of destruction stretched before me. I waited for my dad to rejoin me, like we would do when he'd let me "drive" his big truck—me in his lap, steering, while he shifted and pushed the gas pedal. Instead, he stayed on the ground rubbing his hands together, the quintessential *Harry in deep pleasure* mode.

Does he know I don't know how to drive? I mean, I've turned the steering wheel from his lap and I've played car arcade games, but I think I might need to know something more than turning to the left, turning to the right. After assessing the cockpit, I realized I might need a little more instruction than *go*. "Harry! What do I do?"

"Push the emergency brake down!" my dad yelled back. "Foot on the clutch! That's the one on the left. Move the gear shift to one, then press on the gas. That's the one to the right."

Okay, simple enough. I pressed my foot down onto the left pedal but it hardly budged, so I shoved both of my feet into the pedal as hard as I could then put both hands onto the gear shift. I shoved the gear shift in the general direction of the "1" imprinted on the black knob. It made a terrible grind, metal on metal. But still, movement. I took both feet off the clutch, this time shoving them into the gas pedal. More movement. A lot of movement. I grabbed the steering wheel, hands at three and nine like at the arcade, elbows jutting out to stabilize myself. Neither of us could believe it: the machine and I were marching forward, the forks about three feet off the ground. There was a lever to move them up and down, but I was too afraid to take my hands off the steering wheel. I kept moving down the sandy lane. It was a steep down. How did I never realize that it was downhill?

And then, it was happening.

I was picking up speed, going faster and faster and then I heard a "SLLLLLOOOOOWWWWW DOOOOOWWWWWNNNNN!" coming from behind me. I couldn't look back. It was all I could do to hang on, and with that I realized, I did not know how to slow down, or stop for that matter. How was I going to stop? This was like learning how to ride my first bike. My dad had plopped me into the seat, given me a push, and off I went down the sidewalk on my red two-wheeler, doing great at first, upright, fast, until I reached the end of the sidewalk that spilled out into the intersection. That time had ended in bloody knuckles and a cut on my knee. But this?

How was I going to stop? I was flying past the old Fords, then the newer Fords, then the Chryslers, and over the dogs' discarded hubcap feed bowls—oh wait. This really was just like learning to ride my bike. With my bike I heard my dad yelling the same way behind me from the sidewalk—it was just like now, on the dusty row, except that now I couldn't make out his specific words and I was in a giant machine.

I continued forward. And then, target identified: a few car lengths away, I saw the perfect place to crash. This was a bigger mass than the juniper bush I had used to break my bike speed. Ahoy! Brown wood-paneled Chrysler station wagon ahead. I'm coming for you. The forks torpedoed forward, intent on their death mission. Five feet. Four feet. Three feet. Two feet. One foot. BOOM.

The metal shirked and shuddered as the forks tore through the rear door and quarter panel of the old Chrysler. The impact was enough to bounce me from my position and my feet fell off the gas pedal. I was holding on to the steering wheel, but not in any active captain capacity—simply as a means to not be rocked completely out of the cabin. Finally the engine sputtered to a stall. All sounds and movement stopped. My dad ran up behind me, unusually silent except for the gasps of air. Once he saw that I was still alive, he worked on catching his breath, recovering from a running race he wasn't prepared for.

I sat silently looking at the carnage: forks and car tangled up into a mess. I could have sold that door or maybe that rear quarter panel window. I felt bad. My dad finally had his breath back. Pointing to the brake in between the gas pedal and clutch he said, "There. That's how you stop." So obvious. I climbed down from my perch, legs shaky but happy to find the ground.

"I'm sorry, Harry." A whisper. My voice struggled to get big. He nodded his head and climbed up into the forklift to begin the untangling process while I stood on the sidelines feeling disappointed in myself for disappointing him.

༺ X ༻

As I got physically bigger, stretching upward and outward in sinewy limbs, I would proudly pull parts. My speciality was windshields, where I could use my finesse. I would pry the molding away from the glass, and then with a box knife, meticulously cut into the rubber weatherstripping holding the glass into place. Once thinned, I would take a piece of copper wire, insert it into the material, and run it along the perimeter of the glass. And then came the best part: climbing into the front seat and applying pressure to break the glass free—oftentimes with my feet. My soccer legs were strong and with my body wedged into the seat, hands grabbing a door knob or strap for leverage, I had an unstoppable technique. But the real show stopper was finally freeing the glass and carrying it to the customer's waiting car. Heavy and fragile. Deep breath, wings wide, head down, hoping the afternoon desert wind wouldn't take us for a ride. Please don't drop it, please don't drop it, please… Up the acreage I'd go, the grit hanging in the air and the volume of the wind threatening every step, taunting me to drop it. Not today. Not today. I will collect sixty-five dollars for this. Maybe get a tip when they see how strong I am.

Usually I'd tell myself my same mantra: I am so strong. I can do it. I can do it. …One hot afternoon, in the middle of that same mantra, I was tilting the glass this way and that to reach the destination ahead: a beater car full of greasy-haired men and one mangy German Shepherd. They didn't look too friendly, their eyes squinting with annoyance in my direction, but I stayed the course. Breathe. Don't let the sand suck you into the earth. One more step to the oily pavement. Don't slip. One step, two steps. To the front parking lot. Can they open their back door? Can you slide the glass in place? No cracks. And in! Did they already pay? Can you usher them into the office to pay? Or will they try to take off now that the glass is in the back seat? They see you. Thin child. They know they can outrun you. Are they going to do it? Eyes locked. Who will fold first? They inch toward the driver's door. They are going to make a run for it, aren't they?

I was not big or loud enough to strong-arm them into paying. Quietly, I stepped forward, yanked open the door. "HEY!" they yelled as I grabbed the end of the glass, just enough to slam the door on it. Shards of glass flying. Outrage erupted and I ran, victorious, feeling fine with this form of payment.

Chapter 4
Acts of Bravery

Every day except Sunday, the tall metal gate was unlocked and we hoped customers would arrive. On a good day—usually a Saturday, that holy day of car enthusiasts—customers arrived like a flood, swirling around in the parking lot until our pack of security dogs were locked up and the gates could officially open. They would crowd into the office, plop down on a barstool, and impatiently wait their turn, fingers tapping on my sunny, freshly-disinfected counter, admiring my freshly-swept tiles. Some were respectful of the clean setting, careful to wrap any greasy parts in a red shop towel before taking up space. Others were feral and desperate; whatever part they were after was their ticket to movement. There are no niceties to cloak this type of desperation. Uniformed in our freshly-laundered light blue work shirts, Harry, myself, and a yard guy who went by Mo but whose real name was Leonard, all took orders as quickly as we could, joking with the enthusiasts and barking back at the pack as they shoved greasy old parts across the counter looking for a like replacement. "Just give me something that will work," was the usual plea.

In the early days, this would fill me with dread because I often didn't even know what the part was. I would quickly grab the glob of metal and take a few steps out the back office door looking for one of our parts guys or Leonard/Mo to give me some direction. It was important not to do this in front of the customers, not that I really earned their confidence in the early days, but I knew I couldn't lose face—my pride and my family's livelihood were intertwined with each interaction.

As if retaining my pride wasn't enough, there was something else flickering and sparking within me. It hit me the very first time I sold a part: the confusing power of money. I'll never forget the grizzly old man who shuffled into a bar stool on my first Holy Saturday. He could have been anywhere from thirty to seventy years old; anyone over twenty looked ancient to my twelve-year-old eyes. His wiry beard offered a nest for his breakfast and held remnants of crumbs and grease. His face was smudged with dark swipes of car grease—the official warpaint of the desperate.

"Hi, can I help you?" I offered shyly, shoving a hand in my jeans pocket to steady myself. My other hand moved a strand of hair out of my eyes, a constant battle of maintaining my tween fashion sense against the war of desert wind.

"I need one of these. Or whatever will work," he barked and slid a metal disc my way. A wake of rusty debris followed its path across my recently wiped counter. I made one last pass at my hair, tucking a strand behind my ear. The other hand touched the metal part lightly. What are the questions? What are the questions? WHAT ARE THE QUESTIONS? I tried to remember how to be curious, to suss out what I needed to know.

"What's it off of?" There. There it was. Finally, my brain turned on.

He grumbled something indecipherable. I held steady, squinting my eyes, and waited for more.

Finally it came. "Seventy-five Cordoba," he sputtered.

I glanced at the part again. It had five studs extending upward. Below that was a heavy disc with vents. I quickly considered my clues. Five studs would bolt into a wheel. That part must be related to that. I excused myself from Grizzly with a "Be right back," and headed into our first warehouse. Down the shelves I went, looking for something similar until I hit it. There they were, with a little hand-scrawled sign above the selection: *Brake Rotors*. Ahhhh right. That's what they're called. I scurried back to the office and grabbed the Hollander Interchange book, my most beloved and useful tool. As quickly as I could, I thumbed to Brakes, Front and then to Chrysler Cordoba (I had been working on memorizing cars), and then finally to 1975. My finger traced the dots to its special number: 1515. I smiled and ran back to the brake section of the warehouse, scanning the numbers until I saw it. 1515 scrawled with a yellow grease pen across the metal disc. With both hands I slid the prized brake rotor off the shelf and pulled it tight to my chest so that my body could help my skinny arms transport it. I passed Mo on the way back. He looked at me and my precious cargo. With a nod, he whispered, "Thirty-five bucks."

I continued my journey to the office. With a big smile, I dropped the rotor on the counter next to Grizzly's old one. It was a perfect match. One corner of the old man's lip raised ever so slightly. Methodically, in my best printing, I wrote his invoice and calculated the sales tax. Grizzly dug in his pocket, hoisting out a mix of cash and coins onto the counter, and with a "Keep the change, young lady," grabbed the new-to-him rotor and shuffled out. We didn't have a cash register, so I put the sales dollars in my left pocket and the two-dollar tip in my right. I patted both pockets, the little bumps of cash sending lightning bolts of pure joy through my body.

As the day wore on, I ran out of room. Little bumps of cash were stashed all over my body: in my jeans pockets, socks, shoes, and the waistband of my underwear. When the gates closed at five and the junkyard dogs were freed to protect us, I took my place in the corner bar stool to unearth all the sweaty dollars from their hiding places and stack them with Monopoly-like precision across the counter for the final count. My dad and Mo cracked beers and goofed off. I could barely hear them through the stacks. I counted and then counted again. I knew my mom would want an accurate number. Finally I shared the assessment with the guys, mouthing one number, which my dad countered with another. I slid the difference of our two numbers over to him, and it went in his right pocket. The rest would go home to my mom—mine and my dad's stories aligned for the day—as we mustn't get caught telling a half-truth on Holy Saturday.

When it was not Holy Saturday and the customers did not arrive at 8 a.m., Harry focused on beefing up inventory and scrap materials that could be further recycled. We received endless calls from people with abandoned cars on or near their properties. The wide open spaces of the desert seemed to invite abandonment. You don't need that car, refrigerator, stove, washing machine, grandpa, pet dog? Don't worry. Just leave it. No one will judge.

As the calls would come in for potential scores, my dad would crudely scratch the address on his thick hand, as he knew he would lose any scraps of paper in the wind. He made sure to get the correct street number and some basic characteristics of the street name (the actual spelling of the street always escaped him), and then hopped in the yellow tow truck in search of the loot. On slow days after school, I would often join him on what were *supposed* to be quick adventures but never were. Sometimes, I could even convince my brother to join us. The bench seat didn't have a seatbelt in the middle, so I would expand the belt on mine and cinch both of us in. My dad would toss his seatbelt out of his way—an outlaw too good for safety. Off we'd go, attempting to transcribe the hieroglyphics on my dad's left hand while bouncing up and down over dirt roads. These calls rarely took us to the paved, nicer neighborhoods in town. Instead, we would look for landmarks: right at the cross, left at the fork, go approximately one mile and then make another left at the burnt juniper tree, until we stumbled into an abandoned clump of metal on wheels. Those were the good ones, at least, when there were still wheels and tires present that would allow us to tow with ease. Extra bonus: the owner would be there with a Bill of Sale to make the exchange legitimate.

The three of us had hundreds of adventures like this over the years, but only one remains vivid in my memory: the hunt for the red 1965 MG. It was a strange quest for us, as my dad hated all non-American cars. HATED. It was one thing to be of Asian origin. He, like many car enthusiasts of his generation, despised the tiny, fuel-efficient vessels coming from Japan and China. They lacked horsepower and girth—a smack in the face of the great American car legacy. But, to be tiny and cute and from Britain was too much for him. An atrocity if he ever knew one.

And yet, there we were one afternoon, squinting our eyes at the Bic scrawls on his hand and scouting for forks in the road and burnt juniper trees. A left here, a right there at the big rock, five more miles due west, through the dry creek bed, and it should be… right here. Voilà.

"THERE IT IS!" Ryan pointed to something bright and shiny through the tumbleweeds. Target identified. We increased speed in the unlikely event someone was hiding, waiting to beat us to the treasure.

Oh, and it was cute. So red. So convertible. So hateable, which was clearly communicated to us by the scowl on my dad's face. He grunted obscenities at the monstrosity of a machine. But it had wheels and tires! A sign that it can be ours. I was overjoyed and began the daydream process immediately, placing a very elegant me in the driver's seat, a turquoise silk scarf wrapped around my hair, and dark black Jackie O glasses shielding me from the elements. My god. I am beautiful. Everyone at school will be so jealous. I am almost thirteen. I can fix this car up for when I get my license! It will be mine!

"Hey, get in! Put it in neutral," my dad shouted, and my elegant reverie slipped away. I did as I was told, slipping into the dirty driver's seat, not a silk scarf in sight. My left foot engaged the clutch and I slipped the gear shifter into place. My dad slowly backed the yellow tow truck into me and the MG, the boom and hook lowering to catch us for the final hook up. Maybe it was my dad's hatred for that little red belle or just a lapse in judgment, but instead of stopping at contact, he continued to push. I could hear Ryan shouting from the cab: "Daddy, stop!" Before I knew it, the car was dumped into a deep ditch, stopping only when the back wheels locked into the rutted earth. I kept holding the steering wheel, knuckles whitening as my grasp tightened.

I was not hurt. I was not elegant. But I was mad. Very mad. I eased out of the seat, scrambling over the driver's door to safety and to assess. At the top of the ditch, a tiny Ryan and a hulking dad stood next to each other in silence. The car was too far down in the ditch for the hook to save it. My dad began to pace and mutter. I couldn't hear him through my anger. It seemed he wanted to just leave her there. In the desert. Alone. That sweet little car did not ask for that type of abuse. I was not leaving without her. That was final. A decision had been made.

I walked to the back of her, placing my hands on her trunk, and with all my might, I began to push.

"Rob, it's too…"

Dad was saying it was too heavy or too far gone. That only incited me further and I kept pushing, engaging every stubborn muscle in my body until I could feel it break free from the earth below. We were moving. We were doing it. Inch by inch, I pushed her forward. My dad had to greet me with the hook or else she would roll back and over me. He didn't want to discard a flattened daughter in the desert. I felt sure of that. Well, relatively sure. I kept going and sure enough, my dad scrambled down with the hook to catch her and just as quickly scrambled back up to hoist the boom and my sweet little car upward to safety.

The three of us cruised back to the junkyard in silence with the MG in tow. Instead of the tumbleweeds and macabre yucca trees out the window, I could only see images of me fixing up the convertible for my first car and racing through town with my big, dark sunglasses—the pinnacle of grace and sophistication. I would hear my dad recount the story of my strength to anyone who would listen in the following days. He was oddly proud of me, which helped me stand a little taller. But by the end of the week, his hatred of that non-American machine would get the best of him and I would find her crushed, halved, then quartered in a stack of other discarded cars, scheduled for a shipment to China. My act of bravery and hope for opulence shelved for another day.

Chapter 5
Soar

I can see the whole scene, just as it played out.

We should do it.

I'm scared.

We might not get another chance. They'll be home soon.

I'm really scared. We could die.

My brother and I stand in the middle of the driveway of our new home. I am on skates, holding the handle of our rickety wagon. Ryan is my passenger, clutching his sour blanket for safety. Our new house is on a steep hill looking out to other dusty, steep hills. We've never been perched above the world. Our old life was flat—a combination of meticulously manicured yards and parks with designated bike paths chaperoning us through what was allowed and keeping us off what was strictly prohibited. This new land is not paved and manicured. This new world is so untamed even the roads have no say if they will remain asphalt or become a sand pit. I grab the handle with new intent and hop in the wagon.

Hold on, Ryan. Tight.

He grabs my waist. I can feel the moisture of his stupid blanket against my back. Man, that rag smells. The one thing, after much begging from Ryan, that my mom doesn't meticulously wash.

"Our House" by Madness plays on my cassette player. It's a favorite recording I patiently stole from the radio before we moved away from decent stations. I had placed it at the beginning of the cassette in a series of songs curated for optimal driveway skating choreography—and now, wagon choreography. I inch the wagon closer to the drop of the driveway and squint my eyes to lessen the burn of the afternoon wind grit.

Deep breath.

Turn brain off.

My left skate stabs the ground with force and then quickly retreats into the body of the wagon. The wagon soars past the last flat seam of concrete. We take flight. There's no stopping our velocity now. We are children without brakes. Down, down we go. Ryan and his stinky blanket clutch tighter as I use the handle to steer us relatively straight, or at least away from the extreme edges of the driveway that would dump us into a ravine. I can feel his teeth chomping into my back as we pick up speed. I want to tell him to chew on his blanket instead, but we're going so fast, I can't make the words come out of my mouth. My cheeks are burning from equal parts wind and shame. I underestimated the length and speed. How am I not going to break my little brother when we finally meet the end? The wheels wobble and rattle below us as we continue plummeting to our demise. Finally, I can see where our death plunge will meet the road—it's coming in about twenty feet. I quickly pull out my left leg and then my right, extending my skated feet forward to stretch my legs and then just as quickly, drive them toward the ground, angling my wheels to create some resistance. There's nothing to do now but hope we don't crash too badly. I close my eyes and listen to the rubber scraping off my skate wheels.

Boom.

The next thing I remember is my body face down, stretched every which way in a sand pit, Ryan's teeth mid-bite in my back, grit invading my nostrils. Our rusty old wagon lies toppled on its side, discarded after our ejection. We lie there motionless. Are we dead? Ryan unclenches and squirms off me. No, that's movement. We are not dead. I push myself upright, swatting the dust off my face, and find balance on my skates. We are too shocked by our evident life to cry over our aching bodies and instead begin to laugh, which quickly turns to insane cackling.

Let's do it again.

Who am I to disagree with him? After all, we just gained a bonus life. I right the wagon. Ryan shoves a corner of his blanket into his mouth and climbs in, while I grab the handle and trudge us toward our plateau on my toe stoppers.

"Robyn, did you hear me?"

My sweet nephew taps my arm from the passenger side of the car. We are parked at the scene of the great wagon debacle some forty years later. The pitch of the driveway is steeper than I remembered. How brave we were.

"My dad says you better not write about him."

My eyes scan the vast desert for all the hills my brother and I used to climb together. The steeper the better. We would eventually trade out skates and wagons for bikes and skateboards until age and circumstance would force us to consider individual challenges rather than soar through the days together.

I smile at my nephew, taking in his eager blue eyes so similar to his dad's.

I have to, Ryan. It's the only way I can still love you.

~ X ~

At age four, I lost my Only Child status. Not only did I lose my mom's sole adoration, but I had to share space with a wild, temperamental, completely unreasonable hellcat. My mom and her friends fawned over baby Ryan's white-blonde hair, perfect skin, and effervescent blue eyes. I would redirect their attention to his extra toe, an anomaly, I would point out, confirming he was the Devil and not to be trusted. And yet, there was no denying it. He was a beautiful specimen of a child, especially compared to me with my scrawny limbs pulling me too tall and lean, upward and outward. His physical beauty made it difficult to reconcile his most unangelic behavior. Why is he throwing Legos, again? Why is he hiding in the cupboard, again? Why is he riding his Big Wheel down the street wearing only his Superman Underoos, again? Why is he biting me, again? Why is he yelling at me, again? It was useless to demand answers to these questions. He would simply stuff a corner of his blanket in his mouth and run off—usually half-naked—or, he would lock himself into the special cubby of his bunk bed to play with his imaginary friend, Captain. (I should mention that Captain was an honorary member of our family and accompanied us everywhere, offering commentary on what we should or should not do. Captain was not as wild as Ryan, thankfully, and helped to temper our activities. Where Ryan liked to roam the streets naked, Captain was happier tucked in bed, eager to read stories from Ryan's stack of Dr. Seuss books. I couldn't see Captain, but I liked him immensely.)

༄ ✕ ༄

"Ryan, do you want to play shipwreck?" I had already set sail in our rusty wagon, clutching the side rail, the backyard transforming from lawn to treacherous sea. Toddler Ryan ignored me, standing on the concrete patio next to his *CHiPs* motorcycle, soft belly protruding from his Superman Underoos, his uniform of choice. I tucked the pink crocheted blanket tighter around the dolls I was keeping safe and warm from the turbulent waters and whispered to them not to worry, a helicopter will save us all soon. I tried again, that time deeper into my scene: "Ryan, get in the boat. You aren't safe out there."

The sea rumbled around the half-naked boy as he took one hand off his motorcycle and looked toward the house.

"Captain, tell him to get in the boat! He's going to drown!" I shouted, getting very worried about the tsunami waves growing and growing. There was a pause and a silent communion. Ryan turned to me and scrambled into the wagon. I untucked the dolls to make room for my brother. He scurried under the blanket and I tucked all of them in, safe until the helicopter swooped in for our rescue. "Thank you, Captain, we did it," I whispered with relief.

⸎ ✕ ⸏

I was relieved when Captain moved with us to the desert. I was worried at first that he would stay behind, preferring the lush garden filled with berries and climbing trees to the stark desert, but he got strapped into the backseat of the gold Chevelle station wagon next to Ryan. I wouldn't have blamed him if he wanted to stay—that would have been my first choice. He moved into our first house with joy, accompanying me and Ryan on wagon trips or helping us build forts at the base of prickly juniper trees. Captain was a good sport, traipsing all over the desert, making sure Ryan didn't forget his blanket anywhere or that we didn't get too bloodied up from our various missions. He was the older voice of reason to Ryan's maniacal tantrums and my otherworldly dreamscapes. When I was convinced I was a princess who was placed with the Saunders family for safety from evil space warlords, Captain assured us that my secret was safe. When Ryan wanted to throw rocks at the princess, convinced that she was actually an evil space warlord rather than a benevolent and beautiful princess, Captain stepped in and restored peace.

Somewhat reluctantly, I can only assume, Captain joined us at our second desert house—a dark ranch-style rental further from town, but closer to our elementary school. That house came with a dog, a gift from my dad, because kids in the desert should always have a dog. I no longer remember her name, but she was a mix of German shepherd and cruelty, rescued from the pen of caged dogs at the junkyard. She jumped and snarled every time we entered her backyard lair, the concrete slab of the patio covered in her blood. We learned this was called being in "heat." She was hot and angry. I thought by spending more time with her, gently petting her behind the ears, she would become my friend or at least friendly. But she had other ideas about friendship and assumed an easy dominance over us, jumping and biting, instead of kinship.

After the first several gnaws, Ryan and Captain refused to visit her in the backyard and she was eventually taken back to her prison at the junkyard. We would see her after hours with the junkyard menagerie—a beefy pack of menacing-looking shepherds, Rottweilers, coyotes, and one Doberman. Once the tall metal gates were closed to the public for the night, I would often accompany my dad down the four acres to the far corner of the property to unleash the hounds. There they were, knocking around their hubcaps used as bowls for food and water, and springing up against the chain link fence. I would stick my fingers through the fence so they could smell me. "I am friend," my fingers communicated. "We'll see about that," their noses and snarls communicated back. My dad would unravel the thick chain and with a strong push, the gate would fly open, and out they came: no longer individuals, but a unified army against the world. Dust flying underfoot, the mighty pack twisted and turned, taking in smells, but never losing sight of their goal: office, where food for their hubcaps lived.

With the return of the "heated" dog, the pack took on a new ferocity. In addition to seeking food for their hubcaps, they had a new goal: guarding their sole lady friend. No one, especially us kids, could get near her—her army was quick to jump and knock us down, or worse. Night after night, one of the yardhands would save me or Ryan as the dogs would contort and lunge at us when least expected. Once whisked to safety, we would vow never to leave the office again, but the lure of adventure in the junkyard would override this decision, and we would venture out, eventually finding ourselves cornered somewhere, stuck on top of a stack of crushed cars or trapped underneath the pack. Time after time, we'd have to call out for rescue.

"You are dismissed," said the priest with a hasty, "In the name of the Father, the Son, and the Holy Spirit." The front doors of the church had slammed open, interrupting the final gospel of the day. We were dismissed, but no one moved; no one spoke. I was seated in the pew next to my mom, trying to figure out why everyone was frozen in place. And then I heard it.

"Help me."

It was a whimper. But it was a familiar sound. A familiar voice. I looked up to see my dad in his blue uniform, red cursive *Harry* nametag, and something else. His shirt was soiled with dark stains. Was he carrying something? My memory plays tricks on me now. Sometimes he is clutching what looks to be a bloody shroud. Other times, it is just my dad, the length of his body crying blood and tears.

"Help me." A wail. "Where is my wife?"

My mom and I rushed to him, trailing him to the yellow tow truck that was still running just outside the door. He was not speaking.

"He needs heat," my dad finally said. The truck's heater was blaring and that was when I understood that the blood and mangled shroud on the bench seat was my little brother. I remember hands grabbing me by the shoulders, moving me out of the way. Mouths moving; sirens blaring. I could hear none of it. The world had gone silent. And then the three of them were gone and I was alone.

"I thought it was his blanket," my dad would later recount to the doctors, police, and Child Protective Services. He would recount realizing he hadn't seen Ryan for a while and had looked out the back door. In the distance, down Aisle One, the army of dogs was playing, tossing Blanket into the air, jumping to catch it, each dog taking a corner, pulling, dropping it again, and then dragging it to a new locale. Only it wasn't the stinky white blanket, but the pale body of his six-year-old boy, stripped completely bare by the dogs' teeth and paws, being dragged up and down the length of the junkyard.

In the coming days, everyone would become a dog expert, weighing in on pack mentality; bitches in heat. And soon, it was decided: the four-legged army would face the firing squad. There were no survivors. I no longer remember how long Ryan was in the hospital, nor who took me in while my parents waded through interviews and caregiving and grief. Over a thousand stitches later, the little boy was pieced back together—his ear sewn back to his head; his eyes a new shape. Finally, Ryan was returned to our dark house, house number two, where the windows were never opened, the lights were always dimmed, and voices were always hushed. The blood of the heat had been washed from the back patio. For weeks we would prick capsules of Vitamin E and apply the ointment to his sutured bite marks. Maybe it would help with the scars. At least the visible scars. He would not return to school and would repeat kindergarten at a later date. Captain and Blanket were nowhere to be found.

Chapter 6
Dirty Words and Dirty Girls

Before the move, the boys in our neighborhood were becoming. No longer boys and definitely not men, they lingered in that in-between space of boyhood: obsessed with body parts, both their own and others'. It didn't help matters that cable TV was just becoming affordable and for the most part, adults were scarce in the hours after school. Between the *Playboy* magazines stashed in my friend's dad's bathroom and the constant clicking of grainy channels, we learned that bodies have capabilities other than sleeping, walking, eating, roller-skating, and playing soccer. We, the girls of the neighborhood, kept our findings to ourselves for the most part, fending off the occasional older brother's gropey advances or escaping their spontaneous games of garage strip poker—and in my case, the tentacles of one lecherous old man. The adults seemed none the wiser about our growing knowledge.

So it was a surprise and darkly thrilling during the first years of the junkyard to find calendars of scantily-clad women posted for all to see in the main warehouse.

Sometimes the women were posed with vintage cars; other times with tools. But what remained a mystery is that they were out in the open rather than hiding under a bed or behind a toilet. "Don't look at the trash," Harry would occasionally remark with some discomfort, but would never take down the pictures, worried that his posse might be offended by his prudery.

Women, in the flesh, were scarce at the junkyard, but when they appeared, my god, watch out. They would periodically accompany a husband, brother, or friend—an accessory for an errand. These women, restless and fawning, were not interesting to me. It was the other ones—the ones who came alone with their own tools and calloused hands—that were my sources of wonder. I didn't know women like these in my former life, where most adult women were stay-at-home moms, teachers at school (fierce in their own way, but not this), or the annoying vanilla women at church with their pantyhosed legs, frumpy skirts, matching sweater vests, and soft *nice* voices.

I knew Joan Jett, suited and leathered with a snarl to match; my icon. I knew Debbie Harry, too cool for emotion and tidiness; my other guiding star. Joan and Debbie played on repeat in my bedroom, the power of their music filling my room, but women with that type of coolness were nowhere to be found in normal life. The women I'd see in the yard from time to time, the ones with calloused hands who never wore bras, their breasts dripping down their torsos, side-boob creases visible from muscle shirts cut wider—these women, ranging anywhere from seventeen to seventy, did not cower or take "no" for an answer. They did not put up with any foolery or condescending questions from the yardhands. No matter their age or size, they stood tall as they made their demands, punctuating their requests by squinting their eyes as if proactively preparing to shut down any stupidity. They would light a cigarette and wait for someone to do exactly as they instructed. As a youngster I would hide behind the corner, observing their profound presence and ability to smoke and talk at the same time.

Later, when I was old enough to help these women, I would try to match their strength and posture, but would end up fumbling my words, jarred by their imposing nature. They were breathtaking and I wanted what they had. How does one practice being that strong and cool? I started with the basics: cigarettes. When the yardhands weren't looking, I raided their smoke packs, one cigarette at a time. Slipping into the grimy bathroom, I'd pop one between my lips and stare at my tiny, green-eyed, freckled face in the streaky mirror. It would be a couple more years before I'd light one for real and a few more years until I'd buy Djarum cloves from Porgie's Mini Mart, attempting to light up in the darkness of a park away from ratting eyes. For now I was auditioning, casting the possibilities of leading rebel lady without a cause.

What does she look like with the cigarette shifted to the right side of her mouth? A slight squint of the eyes. Remove that earnestness. Now, say hello like you don't care. *Hellooo*. No, that's too much—too many syllables. *Heeeeyyyy*. Yes, that's better. Do not let your eyes smile. Squint and glare. There you go. Stop standing like you're in line for Communion. Give those legs some room. Shoulders back. Tilt that chin. Now say it again. Out of the left corner. Do not care. *Hey*.

Where we lived, young ladies of a certain age were required to wear a bra whether or not they needed it. There are rules. As a too-tall, too-skinny kid stretching heavenward, my frame left no room for body fat or boobs so I didn't need a bra, really. But again, there are rules and at age twelve my first training bra was selected from an array of boxed garments designed to adhere to this coming-of-age rule from the local TG&Y. Once outfitted to my androgynous body, the triangle outline was visible through my shirts, declaring, "Hear thee, hear thee, this girl is now a woman."

I hated the way the straps cut into my shoulders. I also hated the way the boys at school seemed to keep a running spreadsheet of the bra girls, a constant inventory of those who had titty holders and were now ready to get busy behind the portables. Why we girls didn't gang up on them I'll never understand. We had them in numbers and intellect and yet, more often than not, assumed the position of inferiority, enduring their slights and advances. I wasn't pretty and felt myself slipping away into an in-between state—a strong body, thanks to bike-riding, soccer, and general junkyard mischief, with layers of likes and dislikes that more often than not did not correspond to what my peers were into.

⌣ ✕ ⌢

In sixth grade, I broke a few ribs, a freak accident while doing gymnastics from the high beams in our barn. After a few days of recovery, I was ordered back to school. The pain of my broken torso was excruciating. Every time I moved, I threw up a little in my mouth, but I was secretly thrilled. Not by the puke. That with all the bandages holding me together, I couldn't fit a training bra into the mix. I can still feel the mischievous smirk holding in all the puke as I carefully thumbed through my closet for my first day back at school. This outfit would need to express my coolness. It would need to explain without explaining that I was a kid who was tough enough to break bones, puke without caring, and still ace today's math test all without a bra holding my womanliness in place. I knew just the thing. Tight black jeans and on top, the pièce de résistance: a soft pink, full-zip, sleeveless hoodie. I slowly pulled it all on, careful not to make any sudden movements that would radiate bolts of pain from my torso out. One arm through the arm hole. Then the other. I said goodbye to the layers of bandages as I methodically zipped up and over their bulky constraints, finally stopping mid-cleavage. Only vanilla girls zip all the way up. I took a look at myself in the mirror. Not bad. But I wonder if… a quarter turn to the left… yep, I did it. As I raised my right arm and peeked in the arm hole, there it was: the faint trace of side boob. Today was going to be a great day—broken and pukey, but rebel lady points for the ages.

I remember later that day making my way to the bathroom during recess. A place I would never usually go because who goes to the bathroom at school? Bullies can be found in bathrooms... Or at least that's what the movies told me. But I needed to risk it, to check in. It was one thing to imagine that I was a leading lady in the privacy of my home, but out in the wild, in the chaos of school? I needed to know: had I been transformed? The bathroom was a dank space with two dull bulbs casting more shadow than light. I quickly checked the stalls to make sure I wouldn't be detected by Julie or Danielle, the two girls in my class most likely to make fun of me. The place was empty. I made my way to the mirror hovering over the metal sink. Slowly, I took my index finger and thumb to the zipper of my pink fleece sweatshirt. I tugged it downward. In the mirror, I watched as pale skin transitioned to bandages, the slight outline of my chest protruding. I lingered, keeping the zipper half-mast, just below my breast bone. Spreading my legs ever so slightly, I put both hands on my hips, pushed my shoulders back, and tipped my chin up. Once I knew I was in position, I allowed my gaze to meet the image in the mirror. There she was. Bright and tough. She was not a figment of at-home romanticism. She was real! She was me! If it wasn't for the nausea forcing me to grab the edge of the sink, I would have gladly welcomed Julie and Danielle to see me in my half-zipped glory. I wasn't afraid of their barbs. (That's not true. I was still afraid. But for a moment, it felt great to pretend.)

⸺ ✕ ⸺

In contrast to my work-in-progress as the leading rebel lady, my mom became the patron saint of junkyard-land, silently praying for all of us. She led a dual life, her time split between teaching catechism at her Catholic Church and corralling the many emotions of my dad from her crumb-covered desk in the front office of the junkyard. My mom never swore. She did not reprimand often. But we all knew to keep our voices respectful in her presence to avoid the death glare of absolute irritation. She was better than us. God made that clear. When my brother and I discovered the power of sneering "You can suck ass" as a go-to sibling punchdown, we knew to keep it to a whisper in front of mom for fear of both the wooden spoon delivered at home and the likely—if not equally impressive—wrath of God, which manifested as extreme disappointment, special-ordered by one Karen Saunders.

Even at the junkyard, my mother did not get dirty. Ever. Her nails were always manicured, her dark brown hair kept short and styled for the day. Her typical ensemble was jeans and a sweatshirt. Sometimes, a nice sweater and slacks. Her face was kind and soft—initially. As time went on, worry and impatience began to etch away her compassionate softness, leaving a scowl even when she probably didn't mean it. She would always leave the junkyard at 3 p.m. to pick us up from school and scurry home to watch her favorite soap operas: *Ryan's Hope* and *All My Children*, which she'd taped earlier in the day. With a sigh and a chocolate-marshmallowed Pinwheel cookie in hand, she would plop down in her recliner, silent and withdrawn until it was time to make dinner or take me to soccer practice.

Looking back now, I suspect she was frightened by the overwhelming shiftiness of the place—both the junkyard and the new city as a whole. With the exception of church, which had rules and a dress code, the landscape of our new world was unpredictable—prickly and unforgiving. But at the time, she was just Mom doing what Mom does: making sure none of us got into too much trouble. A full-time job if there ever was one. Her rosary beads got a daily workout from our collective antics.

Aside from my mother, who truly ran operations and kept my dad afloat, we had a Michelle. Michelle was the young wife of Mo, my dad's go-to yardhand at the time. At some point, Michelle and Mo moved onto the premises with their two small children. Their single-wide mobile home was a flash of normalcy against the gritty backdrop, complete with a little garden for the kids and a sweet fence to keep the riff-raff away. I'm not sure how it happened, but one day Michelle was simply in the mix, answering phones, acknowledging customers, and running up and down the aisles looking for parts. She was petite, with blonde shoulder-length hair and a perpetual tan.

At the time, Michelle seemed significantly younger than her husband, maybe in her twenties—this may be time and memory playing a trick on me—and yet, she had many lives etched on her face and in the strength of her carriage. Always in motion, she never rested, lighting a cigarette to reset and then off she went, flicking ash along the way. She didn't mince words and wasn't afraid to toss out a swear word or two when someone went too far. Her armor was thick, the tell-tale sign of a woman who has had to protect herself from an early age. My dad didn't seem to annoy her too much and when he did, she lowered her voice, growled an elongated "Haaaaarrrryyyy" and he backed off. No need to have a long conversation about whatever the offense. Michelle was a great teacher and I would mimic this tactic—her low growl—to mixed results.

Even though I recall Michelle being a godsend and my parents being grateful to have her around, they were visibly nervous around her and any other occasional woman who brought her own tools and voices—my dad especially.

༺ ✗ ༻

Harry loved the women in his life; they kept him safe and connected to the world. He needed them to read for him, to feed him, to pay his bills, to calm him down when his temper got the better of him (usually my job in the early days), and to rescue him when he would go astray (which was often). And yet, his terror could be felt in an instant—a deep fear and distrust that we would just as easily pick up and leave him. It was much easier to reject us before we could reject him.

In some ways, his way of being was completely shaped by women. Harry was never meant to have an ordinary life. When he was a baby, his father moved him and his siblings west from the East Coast to avoid some troubles. A name change ensued; the surname Story became Saunders. But whatever was shadowing my grandfather, it had nothing on the primary source of trouble: my dad's mother, Laura. There was no shaking her. She refused to be left behind and joined the trip to sunny Los Angeles, only to bring her unique brand of drunken trouble with her. Because that's the thing: trouble follows and imprints, sometimes even tagging along for a generation or two to follow. There is no running from trouble even though we try and try and try.

My grandmother Laura, whose birth name was actually Gertrude, died in the 1950s, long before I was born, but her legacy was always present through both family lore and through my dad's actions. She was so present that I could swear I heard her voice in the darker times, telling me not to be afraid or begging me to understand my father when his big emotions led to kicking in doors, breaking windows, raising voices—the root of all of his temperament was her fault.

Laura's mind was a splinter, her body a mechanism for having babies between drinks. After the great lengths she went to—to caravan west with her family—she didn't stick around for long. She eventually abandoned her husband, two sons, and daughter. This would begin a pattern she would repeat several times. Meet man, have baby, leave baby. Repeat. In the coming years, she would abandon a few more children, leaving each kid to be cared for by their respective fathers or the systems designed to catch the unwanted. That was Laura's pattern, but also not unheard of during the years following World War II.

Between 1946 and 1964, the US would birth an average of 4.24 million new babies every year (nearly 350,000 babies born every month, up from 200,000 babies pre-war). The national tendency was to believe in a strong economy, a confidence that there was enough to go around to support growing families. But the truth had less of an optimistic glow, especially for working-class women, single women, newly-widowed women (thank you, War), and the influx of European refugees post-war. Many women found themselves in situations in which they could not provide for their children, unborn or otherwise. Baby Boom, meet the Great Baby Drop, the lesser-talked-about reality of the times. Children's homes, or orphanages, popped up everywhere, a wide net to catch the abandoned.

In my dad's case, one day his mother packed up five-year-old Harry from the family home and began driving out of the city. Some say she ran out of gas. Others claim she met a new man and the kid was inconvenient. What my dad will tell you is that they were driving and then they weren't. He slept in the backseat of the hot car until he heard voices. Drunk again. He knew that much, as her voice slurred and gurgled nonsense. A door was opened and then it was closed. He was left in a boy's home in the middle of the Mojave Desert and never saw his mother again. He would be retrieved by his father several years later, but by that time, the damage was done—abandoned, abused, and scared—a cycle that would become his default. What my father learned from this was: this is what women do. They will hurt you and leave you for others to hurt you.

Laura was an easy target for familial hate. Too easy, and perhaps unfair. Before Laura became defined as a dirty girl, a troublemaker, a breeder, a child-hater, and a drunk, she was just a young girl. Born in 1914, she was raised by what we might consider a troubled young mother who set the stage for what was to come. Laura's mother did what the time period dictated for the poor. She attempted to get by. Survival, although it didn't seem like it, was a choice of sorts, and required marrying, birthing, and, often, widowing. Rinse and repeat, pushing her out of rural self-sufficiency and into tight-quartered apartments with too many mouths to feed and limited resources to do it. Rinse and repeat until the body wore out and resentment crackled and hardened the softer contours of self.

It was this unrelenting cycle of survival that birthed Laura. At first, it seemed she would escape it. Laura was described as a savant with a photographic memory and quick wit. "Too quick; too smart," some would claim later, after the headlines made her fodder for gossip. At sixteen, she was married and with child; the baby would die a year later of syphilis. A second husband came before she was nineteen. Soon, death greeted him by drowning. Alone again, Laura was forced to move in with her mother, her mother's new brood, and her mother's abusive husband, Fred. That was when the troubles really began, and for all the world to see:

Pittsburgh Press, August 9th, 1933: — — Shoots Mate In Fight Over Stepdaughter

Pittsburgh Press, November 11th, 1933: — — Widow Acquitted in Murder; Faces Life of Ruined Hopes

Many causes were cited: jealousy, violence, philandering, and spiritualism (i.e., God made me do it). And who was really to blame for the death of Laura's stepfather? Laura's mother held the discharged gun, but the blame dug itself a deep hole and buried them all. In the end, the specific causes didn't matter—the family was shaken; it was a rattle so deep and hard that there would be no returning to normalcy in mind, spirit, or purpose. Depression settled in with Laura, her trusty and unshakable companion 'til death did they part. As the time period dictated, Laura's mind and trauma went untreated, and the cycle continued: more men, children, drink, and abandonment. She was a casualty of her times and yet a legacy woven into the DNA of those who survived her.

Laura did not remain in the past. Her mark was everywhere. A constant reminder to my dad that love had a door that could be opened and closed: him on one side, his wife—and sometimes us—on the other. I don't know how I knew, but from an early age I could tell that his tight jaw and dark eyes meant fear, and that fear was at the root of his erratic behavior. It was why he flipped dinner tables, yelled, kicked doors, or drove his truck off the road in response to harsh words or general stress. Everything could be taken away in an instant and he would be alone.

It wasn't until I was well into adulthood that I finally understood how much he felt Laura at every turn. I remember the first taste of that deeper understanding, one afternoon in my mid-twenties. I decided to make the trek out to the desert from my then-very-un-junkyard life in Pasadena. I arrived home to find my dad under the hot sun, anxiously gathering tools and handcarts for a junk removal job he had been contracted to do that day.

"I don't feel good about this job," he confessed. Then, "Do you want to see something spooky?" How could I say no to spooky? So, we hopped into his old truck. Me: clean with my new adult life, my junkyard tiara shelved long ago. Dad: dirty blue uniform, standard attire for his scrapping efforts.

We headed out of town, making our way to a long dirt road in the middle of the desert. It was stark, just a lone tumbleweed rolling along the dusty path. Before we found what we had come for, we felt it. A heaviness. It was a place that had seen too much. Dad pulled into the driveway, turned off the ignition. We paused, knowing that we could not unsee nor undo our next steps. He surveyed the land for the scrap metals he was supposed to remove. I followed him toward a deep cut in the earth. Steps led down to where a trailer had been buried. The unmistakable cat piss stench of an abandoned meth lab stopped us from venturing further. Silently, we made our way to the dilapidated house.

The back door was ajar. We called out to warn of our intrusion. It was empty. Dark. The walls were painted black, macabre figures scrawled on all surfaces. Holes had been chiseled into the concrete floor then painted red to make shallow pools, shimmering with fungi and insects.

"Dad, what the hell is this place?"

He shook his head. We stepped over animal carcasses, feathers littering the path. Room after room, we found more of the same: remnants of food, trash, animals. At the end of the hallway, we opened the last door to find a room with light soaring in from the unpainted, unbroken window. Clean pink walls. Discarded toys scattered in all directions. Right away, I realized it was the room of a small child.

"How could she do this?" my dad whispered. "To her kids? How could she do this?"

I turned around. Tears streamed down my dad's face. He was no longer an adult man on a job with his adult daughter, but a tiny boy alone in the backseat of an old car, waiting to be abandoned.

"I'm sorry, Dad," I whispered back. "She didn't mean to hurt you."

Many years later, a few days before his eightieth birthday, I asked my dad what he wanted me to know about him, to which he replied in a high-pitched, nasally squeal, "I'm a bitter man." I met his eyes and smiled, hoping to soften him, to coax out the kind contrast that I know can live within him.

"Cool, Dad. Anything else you want to share?" We were sitting at his kitchen table. I'd come down for the weekend from my home in Salem, Oregon.

His eyes darkened, beady and angry. His body was bloated and injured from a life of manual labor. "No, that's enough."

I had secretly hoped he would say something about the ways in which we had loved him. The ways we created a safety for him to simply be. The times that we laughed, hugged, and even kissed on the cheek. Like that time I attempted to teach him how to read when I was six or seven. He was "reading" a bedtime story to me and Ryan when I realized that the words he said did not match the page. Night after night he would stumble through, telling us about the pictures until I couldn't take it any longer.

"Daddy." I reached out and touched his shoulder. "How about if I read and then I can teach you?" He went silent. I began to cry because the look on his face told me that I had hurt him. To his credit, after that night, he let me read and would even answer my questions when I quizzed him on words or plot.

But instead, as I write this in my middle-age and his final years, I am flooded with regret. If only I had held him more and for longer. If only I had the strength to continue my childlike affections into my teens and then into adulthood. If only I had the capability of having more honest conversations with him, a true listen and response to show him we could be safe for one another. If only I hadn't shut him out as I grew older; my defense mechanism. As I grew older I was unable to take any more misunderstandings or verbal cruelties. Can we spare the heart of another before it goes dark from bitterness?

"Grandmother, was that the best you could do?" I ask the ghost of Laura in the middle of the night, when all are asleep. I ask not from accusation but from wanting to understand. I ask as a fifty-year-old woman on behalf of her eighty-year-old father, after watching him suffer for decades, the smallest infraction setting off atomic explosions within and then rippling out, swallowing those within proximity. I ask now as I've seen enough life play out to see patterns replicated. Conventional wisdom says to accept the past and move on. And that may be true if the future wasn't so reliant on what came before.

The question is a fair one and the ghost of Laura knows it. But she doesn't have answers. Only a question in response: "Granddaughter, is this the best you can do?"

Chapter 7
Exile: Fugitives and Refugees

In the 1970s, as the Vietnam War came to a close, those who had been at war came home or came to new homes. We watched as clusters of Cambodian, Laotian, and Vietnamese families moved into pockets of our neighborhood in Orange County. *Operation New Life,* it was called in the Sunday edition of the *Orange County Register.* Over 130,000 refugees would be placed throughout the country as part of this mission, with a solid third landing in California. Otherworldly. Our new neighbors looked different. Ate different. Lived different. They held multiple generations in one house. As kids, we didn't realize that in many of these cases, these "families" weren't families at all, but groups of people who found each other on the journey to the US, finding home in one another, as their real families were lost to the war. These new neighbors didn't speak our language and were the fodder of neighborhood gossip.

The dads would lean against a mailbox, tallboy in hand, and assess the "fishheads" down the street who occupied several two-story homes, wondering if the newcomers had any rogue grenades waiting to take out the neighborhood. Only one dad had actually served in the war, the rest were excused for various reasons or their draft card was never pulled. They understood war by way of TV and the funny hijinks of *M*A*S*H* (which actually detailed the Korean War) but it was all the same to these guys. To them, Asia was one huge distrustful Communist glob on the map without distinction of borders, culture, or language. America was a bigger glob on the map, responsible for kicking ass and saving the world.

The dads' underlying fear of difference—the gateway drug to racism—was a steady force and it rang true in Harry with one exception: work needs to get done. Who gets dirty work done for cheap? People with nothing left to lose.

Once we made the leap from our safe neighborhood—albeit under the threat of potential grenade attacks—to the desert, the rules of bigotry became fuzzy. I never understood how my dad hired the people he did or negotiated their pay. It's not like a junkyard had an HR department on the ready with tiered salary levels, distinct job titles, or 401k plans. But people would come and Harry would put them to work. If you worked hard, didn't complain, kept your nose clean, and laughed at his dumb jokes, you were in. It didn't matter where you came from or what you were running from. And the truth was, everyone who came to work at the junkyard was running from something.

Enter Vietnam Dan, Wally the Wire Wizard, Clean Don, No-Teeth Frank, too many Jims to count, and Hector from San Salvador. All on the run but stuck. In other words: nothing to lose and therefore, perfect and grateful for the opportunity.

Junkyards—then and now—are notorious for hiring Latino migrant workers under the table, but because of the language barrier, Harry usually "noped" them before they even asked. Except for Hector. No one could deny doe-eyed Hector. In broken English, he claimed he was twenty-one, thinking rightly that he needed to be "of age" to be considered. In reflection, he was probably more like sixteen or seventeen. Over the course of several years as our mutual communication skills improved, Hector would share that he had fled the death squads of San Salvador. His family and friends were lost forever to the violent Civil War. He wanted to live, and that meant going north. Can you live with this particular ache? I watched him labor daily, muscling parts off cars, sweat clinging to the grime coating his body. Customers would give him a hard time for not speaking English. He would simply smile and wander off to the next project. There was no shortage of work. But was this a life? In comparison to a violent death, Hector's answer was yes. He would take this kind of abuse for years before eventually moving on. And like most folks who left the junkyard, we'd never see him again.

The most outrageous of Harry's hires was Wally the Wire Wizard. Wally was the complete package—he had a beautiful but mentally unstable younger girlfriend named Lisa, a blue 1965 Mustang, and a deep knowledge of how things worked. It really didn't matter the subject, he "knew" all: from the inner workings of a bushing to the wide spectrum of interchangeability for a particular car part. His broad smile, albeit missing a few teeth, created ease even if it seemed like he was going to physically jump out of his skin with his constant motion, arms windmilling every which way. He never bathed or stopped talking. "Twitchy" is how I'd describe him. And Wally the Wire Wizard was so dirty we didn't even know what color his hair was. My brother and I would often discuss how he got such a babe for a girlfriend.

"Boobs," Ryan would often whisper when we saw her, and then blush. We would sneak around the stacks of cars to spy Wally and Lisa making out against a car pile—her soft and clean body smashed into his grimy blue uniformed one, door handles jutting into her backside. Over time, the whispers finally met our ears. "Crystal," they said. Ryan and I didn't understand why Wally would be into collecting fake gemstones and why it would be a problem. He seemed more of a muscle car type of guy, but our spying intensified so that we could crack the mystery of this mysterious "crystal."

And although we had guys like Vietnam Dan, who giggled at a high pitch and would often have "episodes" that only his puff of "medicine" could cure—and Clean

Don, whose hand would only stop shaking once he took a swig from a brown bottle he kept under the seat of his meticulous blue Ford pickup—we didn't understand that "normal people" did the thing that Nancy Reagan had warned us about. "Just say no to drugs," the campaign went. And we believed it. Drugs were very bad. All the after school specials confirmed it. Drugs eat your brains and then you become homeless. No one likes you when you do drugs. Your family will disown you. You will lose your job and be very lonely and sick. Little did we know then that that whisper of crystal would eventually become a roar: CRYSTAL METH, bellowing over our desert community in the years to come, decimating brains and lives and eventually, taking my brother with it. A new legacy had begun.

Chapter 8
Love to Love You

Closing my eyes, I remember. My best new-wave-inspired straw hat perched on my bad haircut. The hot desert sun and afternoon wind of grit pelting my waifish body. Twelve-year-old Robyn: crushing hard on Freddy, my dad's new recruit to the junkyard. Freddy had it all. Rakishly thick blond hair, Ray Bans, an orange muscle car, Levi 501s, a love of Bowie, and a swagger like no other. He was a junkyard god. I worshiped him from afar, too awkward and shy to ever talk to him. Every school day I thought my body would explode waiting for that final bell to ring so I could go to work. As my mom pulled into the parking lot, I'd take a quick look in the mirror to check my terrible DIY asymmetrical haircut and sweet, androgynous face, then tear out of the car in search of the Ray-Banned golden boy. Down the dusty rows of cars I'd go, the afternoon wind picking up, threatening to blow my tiny body away. I'd listen for the tell-tale sounds of tools banging against battered metal, knowing that my love would be nearby. And then it would happen. He'd pop up from his perch, smiling.

"Howdy, Robyn!"

A thousand daggers to the heart. A faint smile, a peep of a "Hi" back, and then a full-press scurry through the broken and battered cars, back to the safety of the office, where I could adjust my outfit, check for dirt, and rearrange my hair into a more extreme side part for our next encounter. I was certain these updates to my look made me look edgier, more mature. Or at least mature enough that he would realize I was the love of his life and he should dump his voluptuous girlfriend, Lisa, and maybe take me—a mere but obviously *rad* junior high girl—to his high school prom, where we would coordinate our outfits of black and pink and dance the night away to the Police's *Synchronicity* album, capping the night with my first passionate kiss.

For all the obsession, primping, and strategic placement, I was sadly too shy to ever say more than a few words to Freddy during his short tenure with us. My gangly body and achingly awkward disposition meant that I was simply unlucky in love, both at the junkyard and at school. My school crushes were just that: crushing. To be completely ignored by a peer hurts like nothing else. You should love me, Adam Carney. Look, I am so lovable and cool in unique ways you just don't understand yet. But no matter how much manifestation I attempted, I was met with nothing. No eye contact, no accidental brush of hands as we wrestled our way to P.E. He didn't even attempt to cheat off me in math class like the others. I was invisible. This internal beseeching began in 5th grade and continued through 9th, when I swapped out my Adam obsession for one Greg Toliver, my best friend and secret crush for the ages.

In contrast, the junkyard crushes offered some movement on the reciprocation front. Freddy marked the first in a long string of junkyard crushes where the influx of men and boys were just as broken and battered as the cars strewn about. Easy targets for my Danielle Steel-inspired fantasies (I had been stealing my mom's romance novels around that time—the only education I ever received on sex, love, and European travel). I admired those junkyard boys, mostly eighteen- and nineteen-year-olds navigating their first steps of adulthood. In turn, they loved my admiration, even if it meant suffering through awkward tween chit-chat. This was the epitome of safe distancing before it was a thing. Unlike Adam Carney, the Freddys, Tims, and Bobbys of the junkyard would make eye contact and smile at me, always offering a warm greeting and asking me about school or my bike, a blue beach cruiser I rode everywhere. I liked to imagine they thought I was as pretty as I found them handsome. To be admired, if only a little, was enough for both of us to shine.

If you were to visit the junkyard today, you'd find a shady tree not too far from the dog pen. And if you looked closely on that tree you'd see *RS* + *FK* etched deeply into the bark for all to see. I was a late bloomer for real romance. It would be years before I would have a true, proper kiss with someone I actually liked, years before I'd entangle fingers with someone, that physical gesture that clearly communicates: "We belong together, don't we?" In the meantime, I found a different, more sustaining kind of love to complement my junkyard obsessions.

I found music. And with that—thanks to a new cable channel, MTV—the fantasy of alternative-leaning, trench-coat-wearing boys, often with English accents. My mind was a constant reel of the Talking Heads, Joy Division, New Order, and Depeche Mode. I lived for MTV's *120 Minutes* on Saturday nights, featuring artsy black-and-white videos for clever songs that only fueled my imagination and yearning for more vibrancy. A couple times a week, I would ride my bike over to the record store on Main Street to flip through vinyl and look at posters. Rarely did I have money to buy anything. It didn't matter. Being in the space was its own vehicle to other worlds. Flip, flip, flip. Fast enough to see as many album covers as possible, but slow enough so that I could stay and listen to whatever Jay, the clerk, played on the almost-as-big-as-me speakers. Jay was a recent transplant from Orange County, too, and mostly played ska and punk bands from the beach cities.

Nights were spent choosing the perfect album to match my melancholic longings, dropping the needle onto the vinyl and scurrying out my bedroom window so I could lay underneath the stars on the front lawn (the only patch of green on our street). The cool, wide bristles held me steady under the limitless sky as the Smiths sang me a lullaby. *Please let me get what I want,* indeed.

Morrissey understood and shared my dreamy mopiness. And oddly, so did my brother. At the time I really started getting into music, Ryan was eight to my twelve. Although we fought with fists and kicks during the day, once night and loneliness rolled in, we were each other's confidante and best friend. Most nights, he would find me on the front lawn singing along to a sad band. Without a word he would either lay down next to me on the cold, spiky grass or would simply grab my hand, pulling me up so that we could sneak our bikes—my blue beach cruiser and his tiny yellow BMX—out of the garage. Off we went, pedaling to more remote parts of town, pavement to gravel, gravel to dirt roads, and then finally into the dark desert, carving our own trails between junipers and sage. No lights or helmets (we didn't know they were a thing).

During these escapades, we spoke little, humming our favorite songs instead of talking. We'd take turns leading, quietly careening into ravines and grunting up soft bluffs until the light of the moon was replaced by the rising sun. That was our cue to either get back home or check our pockets for any extra change so that we could share a plate of biscuits and gravy at the diner before my dad woke.

On most Saturday mornings, we would take up residence at the diner after our ride. We made sure to pilfer the couch for discarded coins before leaving home. I usually had some spare dollars from my weekly junkyard sales. Between the coins and dirty bills, we had enough for not only biscuits and gravy, but also cups of hot chocolate with extra whipped cream. Even though the whipped cream gave it away, we felt so grown up sipping from the brown mugs just like all the old-timers drinking coffee in the other booths. Those Saturdays were sacred. Bikes leaned up next to the window, mugs in hand, and the sun waking up, soon to warm the desert. There wasn't much to say, although we would inevitably end up giggling and snorting our whipped cream, catching each other's eye in that shared sibling communion as if to say, "Can you believe we're getting away with this?" Harry and Karen would never allow us to run that wild in the middle of the night and celebrate with hot chocolate. Or at least, that's what we thought. If my dad knew, he never let on. He would find us at the diner most Saturday mornings assuming we were overachievers, up early for work at the junkyard rather than insomniacs trying to ride off the edge of the planet. "Look at these kids," he would brag to the old-timers scattered about the brown booths. "They can't wait to work." The old timers nodded without looking up, our secret gravy adventure safe for another week.

Chapter 9
Bananas

"Dammit!" Peeling a banana should not be this hard. I tug at the stem, attempting to break my banana free, only to continue to mangle and bruise.

"Do it from the other side. Didn't Grandpa teach you that?"

I glance up at my now twenty-year-old nephew and squint my eyes, wanting to dismiss his advice merely on source. But of course, I do as Justin says and take my thumbnail to the bottom where it peels with ease. How am I fifty years old and just learning this technique?

Uncharacteristically, Justin smiles at me without gloating. He is not keeping score at the moment and that feels great. "Grandpa taught me that," he repeats. "So I don't waste food. He didn't teach you?"

We are in the desert. Just the two of us. My husband and daughter stayed home in Oregon, as this place is not part of their story. It's been years since our last visit and we are both nervous balls of our own confusions, stray memories leading every which way. *This is where... this is why... do you remember... this one time... it was always like...* Every corner has a story. I try to tell the funny ones so that Justin can dig deep and find the humor in his own story: of how he was loved, of how he was silly. He forgets sometimes, focusing only on how he was angry; how he was hungry.

"Nope, your grandpa definitely did not teach me that. BUT, I *totally* have to show you something he did teach me." My *totallys* get wild every time I land in California, springing forth in every sentence. It's as if my tongue knows it can finally relax and just be, *totally*'ng through sentences rather than injecting any precision of language. It's an emotive communication device known only to native speakers, declaring agreement without sharpness of judgment.

We finish up our bananas, pancakes, and coffee—my favorite hotel fare, especially now that I know the Harry Saunders banana trick—and hop into the car. Down Main Street we go, over a bridge, and then left onto what's still a dirt road all these years later. The poor rental car gets a workout over the washboard road. We sway and lose traction as I pick up speed.

"To the right is where my elementary school bestie, Raychelle, kept a storage container. It had ATCs. We would ride our bikes here and then break in and grab them. We rode all over this desert and the golf course," I say in my best tour guide voice. Justin nods approval, especially on the golf course detail. We continue on a little further, until I make a full stop. "This is where Grandpa taught me my biggest lesson."

Justin looks out the window. We have pulled off the side of the road into a small clearing. He looks back at me with a confused curiosity. There is nothing to see but desert. How could this be the ONE most important lesson? I pause for a few moments, taking it in, and then I close my eyes, conjuring the cold and excitement of one Saturday morning long ago.

My dad and I had finished up our biscuits and gravy and our respective coffee and hot chocolate at the diner across the railroad tracks. It was still hours before the gates would open for Holy Saturday and I don't think he knew what to do with me. I was almost thirteen —a year into my junkyard tenure—and although my memory banks were overflowing with makes, models, and numbers, my physical strength wasn't quite up to par to be of assistance to him for the morning rituals of yanking tires off wheels or moving core engines to the scrap pile.

He grunted and snarled in response to my rapid-fire tween commentary about our world at large. Harry Saunders did not have the prerequisite patience for the intricacies of Duran Duran videos. Finally, he had too much and snapped.

"Take these. Go. Practice." Incoming. I grabbed the set of keys lobbed through the air. Was he saying what I think he was saying? He didn't stick around for conversation so I was left with a choose-your-own-adventure decision:

Choice A: Retreat to the office. Make hot cocoa and put keys on hook next to coffee cups.

Choice B: Unlatch front gate. Make way to blue Chevy pickup. Use key to unlock door. Insert key into ignition.

There was no hesitation. Choice B. I made my way out of the fortress, slid into the truck, and tucked my seatbelt into its receiver. Safety first. My feet tapped down at the floor. Cool. I could reach the gas pedal and the brake. With that knowledge, I inserted the key into the ignition and turned. The truck rumbled to life. Where would I go? How would I do it? I thought about all the times I'd ridden with my dad, his hand shoving the gear shift into place, his feet alternating between going and stopping. How hard could it be?

My right hand yanked the shifter to D. We drifted forward. Okay, that wasn't so bad. I tapped on the gas pedal ever so slowly and pulled out of the parking lot, aiming the big truck to the left, and then another left, and then another. It was only 6 a.m. so there weren't any other cars on the roads—dirt or paved—just me and Big Blue. We were free. I quickly gained confidence. Too much of it. My feet no longer gingerly tapped at the pedals. Instead, my right foot was a steady source of pressure. We were flying. We were turning. We were… uh oh… Red and blue lights flashed behind me.

"PULL OVER!" bellowed out over a speaker. We were in big trouble.

With a jab of my left foot, I floored the brake, swerving into a sandy bluff. It was enough to freak out Big Blue, her engine overwhelmed by my ineptitude. She stalled and I sat still, trying not to freak out myself as the officer made his way to my window and tapped. Did he think I was an adult? I was scrawny, but tall for my age. I sat up straight, trying to take up an adult portion of space. I didn't know I was supposed to roll down the window and instead flung the door open and hopped out to meet my fate.

"Ma'am, you're going a little fast," he said politely, a kindness I didn't deserve. "I clocked you at forty-five around that last turn." How long had he been following me? Note to self: learn to use mirrors. I know when I'm beat, but I couldn't bring myself to speak; not even a *sorry* made it past my lips. Probably because I was not sorry. I remained mute, but stood taller. He added, "You're Harry's kid, aren't you?"

I nodded.

"Okay, let's get you back. This time, slower around that corner." The officer wandered back to his car, flashed his lights one last time, and waited for me to get back into the truck. What? He wasn't arresting me? My body was shaking as I turned the key. Big Blue was ready for action again as we pulled out of the sand bluff and back onto the potholed road. Slow and steady. A right, then another right, and another until we were back to the junkyard where my dad waited for me out front. I parked across the street, unsure if I would need to make a quick getaway. The cop rolled down his window, barked something at my dad, and then rolled on.

"What did Grandpa do?" Justin is waiting for the inevitable Harry Saunders meltdown he knows well. We're still parked in the sand bluff, the scene of my first major crime.

"He told me to get back in the truck."

In lieu of a meltdown, my dad calmly walked to the passenger side of the truck and hopped in, waiting for me to assume the driver's seat again. My hands shakily turned the ignition, my feet jabbing at the gas pedal.

"Let's do it again," Dad said, waiting for me to let off the brake before providing the next instruction. Turn by turn, we made a left, then another left, then another. Each one smoother and slower than the last until we reached the sand bluff. He didn't say a word, so I simply turned around and made the series of rights back to the junkyard, finally parking in the greasy lot. He jumped out and sauntered off to work. I took a moment to collect myself and then followed suit.

Justin begins to laugh. This is not the grumpy Grandpa he knows.

"Justin, your Grandpa didn't always get things right."

He smirks at this obvious truth.

"But one thing he taught us is that no matter the crime, we could always make a different choice the next time. We could always do better and he would never hold any of it against us. It's why I love you unconditionally and never give you grief," I tease and playfully punch him in the shoulder.

But it's true. I look across the desert to the steel fence outlining four neat acres in the distance, now standing guard to someone else's dreams. It's still there—two green warehouses, forklifts, scrap heaps, and a shady corner for junkyard dogs. A fortress protecting so many hopes, fuck ups, and do-overs. Justin had never seen the junkyard until then, even though the trajectory of his life was birthed here.

~ X ~

In the early years, we had a bulldozer, its scoop outfitted with a several-ton weight used to crush cars to a quarter of their shape. One day when I was about thirteen, I was goofing around and scrambled from the driver's cockpit into the scoop as my dad drove forward, toward a pile of cars he intended to flatten. In my little perch, we marched powerfully across the asphalt to the row of car victims awaiting a smashing. Me and the machine and Dad. We were one. Giddy. Ready to tackle anything. Until something even more powerful clutched at my chest.

A sensation growled in my chest. It said, *Something is wrong. Very wrong.* Then it yelled: *MOVE*! I shot out of the scoop's cavern, pulling myself upward and back on top of the scoop. Just as I regained balance above, the several-ton weight shifted below me, smashing into where I had been perched only seconds before. A cold sweat eclipsed the growl and I choked back a sob, a sob like both a consolation and a reprimand for being so dumb. I waved to my dad to lower me.

I have thought about this incident almost every single day since it happened. Each time, I remember a detail more clearly. My sweat, racing heart, light blue shirt with a "Robyn" badge; the shade of bulldozer yellow; the absolute certainty of love for my dad and not wanting to hurt him by getting hurt; the smell of oil, gasoline, and grit rising from the hot asphalt. In some memories, I can only fixate on the heft of that huge iron ball tucked into the scoop, while in others, I remember the lightness of escape as I slipped through the body-sized crack and hoisted myself to freedom, the weight shifting and trembling below me.

Such is the lesson of weight as it pushes its solidness around. Can we bulldoze forward or will we allow the monstrosity to crush us? I was shown how expendable life can be from a very young age. I watched how cars once whole could be halved and then quartered. I listened as people fled horrors or created them—their minds and bodies trapped in time and consequence. How names were changed and histories erased. I saw how the mounting bills and pressures of family life stopped my parents in their tracks—no time for choices or actual living. I felt the crushing weight of it all. Would it take me out, too? Was there a choice?

I remember this when I gasp for air in the middle of the night, waking from another nightmare in the bulldozer scoop. I wonder what will become of my children—a daughter and a borrowed son. What have they inherited from me? Do they know how to make choices? Do they know how to pay attention; to listen to their heartbeat? Can they feel my heart rooting for theirs? Do they know what it is to feel safe and to be loved?

Listen, the weight whispers. *Just listen.*

I am listening.

Shhhhhhh, let them wiggle and be free.

Chapter 10
It's On

"It's on! Hurry!"

My mom is beside herself with anticipation, nestled into her favorite brown recliner, afghan pulled up tight for a night of love and devastation. I run from my side of the house, dragging a favorite blanket to join her, stumbling over the tail end of fabric in my haste. I jump onto the couch, pulling my legs under me.

"Ready. Did I miss anything?"

She shakes her head at me, so focused on the TV I don't think she's even blinking or breathing. It's November 13th, 1988, the first day of the *War and Remembrance* mini-series on Channel 7. It's the follow up to *The Winds of War,* which aired a few years earlier. My mom had read both books of those same titles by Herman Wouk and now, starting today for the next two weeks, it was coming to life on her TV with an all-star cast in her living room, next to a roaring fire, endless bowls of popcorn, and me. At fifteen years old, I lived for these epic stories with equal fervor. World War II? Romance? Violence? Heroics? Sign me up.

Mom in her chair, me on my couch, Dad already showered and in bed, Ryan tucked into his bunk bed. No complaining. No whining. Silence from 8 p.m. until 11 p.m. with the exception of the occasional sob as my mom's sense of empathy got the best of her and tears would stream down her face, just as a scene would cut to a commercial. Her tears would incite my tears and we would spend the commercial break recovering, getting all the emotions out so that there was room for more when the flashy theatrics resumed. From my perch on the couch, I had watched my mom's emotions pour down her face again and again over the years. Peeking through the holes of my crocheted blanket, I could safely observe her unabashed yearning and sadness as she donned the stories as her own.

The first time I saw her overcome with "love," her face softened, cheeks slightly blushed, green eyes dazzling and wet, mouth in a controlled smile, hands clasped in her lap. This was mom watching *The Sound of Music* when Captain Von Trapp, played by the dreamy Christopher Plummer, first gazed at Maria, played by the most beautiful woman on the planet, Julie Andrews. *The Sound of the Music* was the first time I saw what love could be via my mom's reaction, but it had nothing on the view through my blanket holes when THE Richard Chamberlain kissed Rachel Ward in the mini-series *The Thorn Birds*, a tale of forbidden love between a family priest and a beautiful, spunky woman in the Australian Outback.

Always the romantic Catholic (who doesn't secretly crush on a young, handsome priest?), my mom's face flushed from a soft pink to a solid fuchsia, tears in a constant river flow. *The Thorn Birds,* which was based on the 1977 novel by Colleen McCullough, had the added glamorous benefit of special guest appearances from Christopher Plummer and Barbara Stanwyck. Stanwyck, in particular, was a household favorite, as she had been an acquaintance of my great-grandmother when the two worked together at Paramount Studios for Cecil B. DeMille back in the day. Proximity to Hollywood connections is a Southern California obsession—a couple degrees of separation from greatness can make even the most tedious life hum along with hope. We were no exception.

Between mini-series, daily soap operas, and the juicier evening ones, millions of people across the US, if not the world, tuned in to these stories during the 1980s. There's no denying that the plots, even the most absurd, shaped how we viewed romance, family life, fashion, history, and even the concept of boss babe, a shoulder-pad-laden work in progress. Even if you weren't a story hound, it was impossible to escape the influence. Technology was morphing again in efficiency, and it was now within reach to own a VCR to record, watch, and share shows at a later date. If you couldn't watch something at the time, you simply set your VCR's timer and voilà: slightly-delayed entertainment for when it was convenient.

In addition to the epic mini-series based on historical romances, my mom lived for the soapy canon. All the weekly evening greats: *Dynasty, The Colbys, Falcon Crest, Flamingo Road, Dallas, Knott's Landing*; a special shout-out to her daily mental retreats: *All My Children* and *Ryan's Hope*. Mom in her recliner, either cozied under a blanket or knitting one—hands kept busy by crochet needles moving in and out of yarn—transported to far-away lands that did not include junkyards, grease, bad language, and crusty old men wanting something or throwing temper tantrums.

I always wondered what she thought about in the cocoon of her blankets with a Pinwheel cookie in hand. Did she imagine herself in a tight and shiny gown in the warm embrace of one of these dapper fellows? Or in one of the many luxurious mansions instead of our modest one-story home, which wasn't too shabby by desert standards, but paled in comparison to the opulence on TV? Did she imagine how great it would be to have a housekeeper make us dinner rather than toiling in the kitchen herself—only to be met with complaints from her family of picky eaters, one an annoying, sporadic, and pretentious vegetarian? (Hint: that was me.) Was it enough escaping into an imaginary life for an hour or two a day to endure the less-than-glamorous life around her? Was it enough to vicariously experience passion through the screen when her own husband would walk through the door, see a steamy love scene on screen, and remark, "They just want sex. What trash." Did she feel shame for wanting more, yet knowing that it wasn't going to happen in real life? Was she repulsed when my dad fell asleep in his recliner, freshly showered, belly protruding from his white undershirt, pajama bottoms practically pulled up to his armpits, short hair askew, and snoring as if breath was a near impossibility? Was this the life dreams were made for? Was this the life she would have chosen for herself—that she did in fact choose for herself? Or maybe this *was* enough. I would ask her over the years both indirectly and directly. She would evade a clear response every time, her sense of duty and obligation tightly coiled, unwilling to be unraveled for what it might mean to choose differently.

As my life shakes out, I share less and less with her to avoid the guilt of finding my own glimmers of happiness. I share less to avoid misunderstanding and judgment for all the poor decisions I will learn from. I share less to avoid adding to gossip fodder that I can overhear on whispered phone calls to friends and relatives. I share less to hold on to my privacy and my own story. That night in 1988, I watched my mother watch the TV for steamy love, checking my own memory banks for the other kind of love, the pure one that only a mother can provide. The one who walked me to school in the mornings when I was little and who couldn't wait until it was time to walk home with me; the one who sat down at her sewing machine, and with such care, busted out new clothes for herself and for me; the one who cared for her own mom even when she was unable to reciprocate; the one who made chocolate chip cookies because that's what moms do; the one who cried when my dad spanked me so hard I couldn't walk and then later forgot the memory to protect us both; the one who wanted us to feel love even when she wasn't always able to demand the same for herself.

In the opening pages of *The Thorn Birds*, a myth paints the backdrop. It begins with the legend of a little bird who will sing just once in its life, more sweetly than any other bird or being on earth. The little bird leaves its nest in search of a thorn tree—never stopping until the tree is found. And then, once found, it impales itself on the longest, sharpest spine. As it dies in complete agony, the little bird finds its voice, singing the most pure and beautiful song. The entire world stops to listen, and if the legend is to be believed, even God in his heaven cracks a smile with the knowledge that only the best can be bought at the cost of great pain.

Chapter 11
車で (by car)

My first car that had a set of keys, four wheels, and belonged solely to me was a 1983 Honda Civic, a four-door sedan. She was no small miracle and was the third love of my life (after my two bikes).

And she had everything stacked against her.

First, she was Japanese, a lonely foreigner in our world of muscle cars and vintage American clunkers. Second, she was newer than our usual inventory, which meant street value, which meant I prayed daily that she would not catch my dad's eye and his need for quick cash. Third, her front end was completely smashed and her engine and transmission were suspect.

At almost sixteen, I was a realist. By this point I had loved up on several cars, taking great care to clean and claim them for when I got my driver's license. The more I took interest in a car, a collective realization would hit my dad and the groupies: destroy or sell. I tried not to take it too personally when the cars were sold (with the exception of a 1964 ½ Mustang—promised for years and then one day, vanished). I understood the need to pay bills. However, there was no getting around the devastation to my heart when the guys jammed forklift forks through the windshield or—worse—through the fleshy side panels or doors of the machines I loved most. Watching forks mangle the very structure of those cars was too callous to rationalize.

Strategy and special ops were needed to protect my little Honda. Safeguarding our love required me to play it cool, to not show any interest in her before she could realistically become mine. To divert attention, I would openly discuss a 1964 Plymouth Valiant on Aisle Two, eight cars down on the left side. She, too, was a looker with her four door, boxy sedan lines. Plus, she was universally hated by my dad and his groupies because she had a 170-cubic-inch Slant-Six motor rather than the more powerful, dude-centric, obnoxiously loud V8. I found her elegant in her more refined horsepower potential. Surely this was enough to lure the forklift arms of death toward the Valiant rather than my beloved Honda Civic.

The clock ticked forward and I kept waiting for disappointment; to find sweet Honda smashed in a pile like all my other metal love interests. I hesitated on cleaning her interior or even mentioning her in conversation. As my birthday loomed, the Plymouth Valiant cover strategy seemed to be working and I became more bold in my activities. Honda lived on Aisle Three, four cars down on the right. I'd make my way to her, looking out for spies before ducking into the backseat with a small plastic bag to collect trash and general debris. With each visit, I would lovingly take a shop rag to a new section, wiping off dust and the usual car crumbs. I steered clear of the temptation to wipe down her exterior—she needed to remain as dirty as possible on the outside so as not to raise any suspicion.

And then things started to happen. With great caution, I began to order parts from other junkyards for her. New fenders, hood, grill, and bumper—check. The guys from our extended junkyard network were overjoyed to help me out, hooking me up with many of the parts for free. Finally, young Robyn was gonna drive her own car. This was a time of celebration. Once the parts showed up, there was no going back. It was happening and no one was going to stop this love connection. We began to talk about this relationship in the open; the inner and outer work she would need to overcome. My mom rattled off practicalities about the cost of insurance and gas and being a person who could be trusted with such a large responsibility. I didn't want to rock the boat and counter that if they could leave me to run their business while they went to Las Vegas on vacation, surely I could be trusted to drive a car from point A to point B. I kept my annoyance to myself. My dad actually seemed happy to see me—so happy and didn't say a mean word about Honda's country of origin.

And then one day, the forklift moved her from Aisle Three to the front of the junkyard. My dad backed the good old yellow tow truck to her, connected, and then led her away. She was allowed to roll. She was not crushed or sold. Off to Jack's Body Shop (an old friend of my dad's) where she was finally treated with the dignity she deserved. I was asked to look at a color chart and choose whatever hue called to me ("Choose something that screams" was the actual instruction from my dad). I wanted her to look like my first bike that my dad had built for me—deep blue and shiny.

I collected stickers for her back window and a tiny skeleton to dance from her rearview mirror. More parts were gathered and installed. Into the paint booth she went for her external transformation, perfumed in chemical vapors and layered in color until she shimmered. Next up, her internal makeover. Against the collective hatred for these tiny, efficient machines, Mo and the groupies dove in, wrenching her back into functional existence.

Finally, time shifts: I am sixteen. A key is put into my palm.

I slide into the driver's seat, close the door, and dream of where we could go. Far. Far. Away.

Drive. To school. To work.

Drive. Everywhere but school; work.

Drive. Out of the town. Onto the highway. Down, down the Cajon Pass, through the fault lines—cracks separating desert, forests, and valleys.

Drive. Down, down, and away. To the city. Any city. To people, ideas, shapes, music.

Drive. Far and forward.

I turn the key.

She rattles and hums to life. Life! Life! Life!

I roll down the driver's window to let the hot summer air move through and I pull the gear shift into drive. I can see my dad watching me through the windshield. Is that a smile on his face? She lurches forward. I can hardly breathe as I make a right onto the road, past the VW junkyard to my right, past the Jeep junkyard to my left, dodging potholes of the poorly-maintained road. I reach over and roll down the passenger window. The afternoon heat and wind strike my face, whipping my fine hair into knots. I roll the windows back up to preserve my hair only to be too hot within a minute or two. Who cares? Be wild, I instruct myself, and reach over again to roll down the windows, the wind tornadoing my hair in an instant. Up and down the streets we go, the familiar neighborhoods taking on new shape and color from this vantage point. *Go faster*, Honda urges as we round bends and forge our way out of the familiar residential streets.

This is it. This is what I've been waiting for since we moved to this place. I drive past the city limits, the road narrowing as the elevation begins to drop and the juniper trees give way to softer chaparral, brown to green, birds everywhere fluttering high, quail scurrying low. An hour goes by and the heat of the day slips away, replaced by a cooler breeze. I keep going another hour, until I can't see any patches of desert. Finally, I pull off to the side of the road and push the shifter into park.

Who knows how long I sit there. Long enough for the sky to turn dark and the hot air to stop strangling me. I take a deep breath, my lungs happy to fill with ease—an ease I hadn't felt since I was a little girl. And then the tiniest of tears forms in my eyes. Before I know it my body is shaking with sobs. I run my fingers over my matted hair, careful not to dig into the knots too deeply. I look in the mirror. Wild green eyes stare back at me.

"You've been so sad," I tell her and take a hand to her cheek, stroking the flush away. "We're going to be okay now. Don't worry." She slowly smiles back at me. We know what it is to be free. We know it is the only way forward and the only pursuit that matters.

༺ ✕ ༻

Wheels meant that I no longer needed to rely on my dad to take me to school. Up until that point, I would begin every morning yanking a hard-bristled brush through my tangled hair, scowling at my face in the mirror just outside my bedroom. My dad, hopeful to avoid my wrath, would tiptoe in with a McDonald's sausage and egg McMuffin, sliding it across my makeshift vanity, and say "Five minutes" in a sing-song annoyingly fake voice. Dammit. Five minutes to eat and detangle. The salty McDonald's offering only intensified my frustration, but I could never tell my dad that I was a vegetarian or that I hated McDonald's. His offering was generous and I felt terrible for hating it. I'd shove a bite in, grab my books, and head out the door to the next step of my morning process.

Having my own wheels meant I didn't have to hop into my dad's bright yellow tow truck for my ride to school.

Up until that point, my ride to school would start with a sweep of my hand over the seat before I hopped in, sliding the random peanut wrappers and grit to the floor of the truck. We'd rumble out of our neighborhood, down the main drag, and finally turn onto Maple Street. I could feel the stares as we roared to a stop in front of my high school, everyone eyeing the swaying boom in the back. The kids with cars gathered in the parking lot to smoke or make out until the last bell shooed them indoors. I refused to be embarrassed by my grand entrance or the middle-aged dad with Brillo'd hair and an already-dirty blue uniform next to me. I grabbed my books, muttered a halfhearted thank you, and slammed the door. This was the one part of the day I stood my entire five-foot-nine stance, chin up and shoulders back. The rest of the day's antics would wear me down, but this march from tow truck to first period, across the smattering of high school cliques, required a warrior and I refused to falter.

So it was a great relief to avoid McDonald's and the big yellow beast. The hair detangling process was still unavoidable, but instead of a force-fed breakfast and hating myself for hating morning Dad and his high-pitched, fake-friendly good morning tidings, I would elegantly slither out of the house and into my sweet little blue Honda. A gentle turn of the key and she would softly rumble to life. I'd take a moment to warm her up and adjust my books so they wouldn't slide off the gray cloth seats as they were apt to do over our pot-holed roads. I'd pop the Cult's *Electric* cassette cued to play "Wild Flower," the best hype song I could find for my mornings. A quick glance in the rearview mirror. Yep, I'm ready. Out of the neighborhood, down Main Street, a right onto Maple, and a quick shot into the parking lot. It was only a ten minute drive but in those ten minutes I could gather myself, feel like a real adult. At first, it felt great to arrive, gather, and then make my way to class. Look at me. I am so responsible. I am practically a grown-up. I'd lock my little car and shove the key in my bag. But soon I realized, I had the greatest tool of freedom at my disposal. Why, oh why, was I using it to get to a place like high school?

And so it began. Where could I go between 7:15 a.m. and 3 p.m. every day before I had to be back at the junkyard for my afternoon session? I could drive around town or hide out at a local park. I quickly vetoed that. Small thinking. Plus, one of my parents' spies would see me. How did they become so well-connected? Back to the bigger question: where to go, where to go? The answer became obvious as soon I slid behind the wheel. Out of the neighborhood, down Main Street, past the high school and onto the 15 Freeway southbound. I could go just to the last exit before the desert gave way to Cajon Pass. This is what I would tell myself every time. Just to the edge. But then the edge would come and I couldn't bring myself to take the offramp. Down the steep pass I'd go, settling into the middle lane, holding the steering wheel steady against the heavy winds needling my car from every direction. The offramps were few and far between, not that I could make myself stop. New freeway choices would present themselves, arteries of cars pumping life into our adventure. East? West? No—not yet, at least. These first excursions felt like a torpedo beyond my control. I needed to get home. My real home. Ninety miles later, I would find myself parking in a quiet neighborhood in Laguna Beach, locking the car, then making my way across the Pacific Coast Highway to the sand and the ocean.

It was at that beach that I had learned to swim into the waves, scaring my mom by staying underwater too long until she just got used to it and refused to save me anymore. We would come to that beach most Saturdays in my childhood and even sometimes during the week, visiting my dad who worked up the street. Long ago, my dad had filled a 55-gallon drum with sand from that same beach so I could have my own Laguna in our backyard.

Even though I was a lonely sixteen-year-old by herself on a school day, I didn't stick out when I'd visit Laguna during those ditch days. Laguna was known to attract wanderers and artists and Hare Krishnas. What was one more young girl to the mix? I would peel away my black Doc Martens and dip my toes into the water. But rather than stare out at the neverending Pacific, I would turn back to the shore, searching out the extraordinary homes climbing the sharp cliffs framed with palm trees, California oaks, and laurel sumacs. Those hills and the architectural barnacles were all I needed to restore my imagination—nature and human ambition intertwined to create something more than mere survival. I felt a kinship with this magnificence, or maybe if not sisterhood, I felt hope. That would do.

And with that, I would make my way back to my trusty Honda and floor it back to the high desert before my 3:30 shift began at the junkyard. Back to the oil-slicked parking lot, ready to pretend that nothing special happened in the day. Back to trying—always trying—to help frazzled, grimy men find parts for cars that would never see the ocean or even the next town over. I may have been a high school ditcher, but my work ethic for my family was strong.

It wouldn't be long before I ventured in other freeway directions to follow my growing curiosities. I learned about Jane's Addiction in 10th grade chemistry class from Gina Smith. Two years my senior, Gina was easily one of the smartest kids I had ever met. But on first introduction, she was easily one of the most intimidating kids I had ever met: "Skinhead Gina," who later explained that she was actually straight edge, an important distinction she didn't bother sharing with most kids so she could keep up her reign of intimidation.

Gina loved to learn, read, and see live shows. I had never met anyone like her—so fierce on the outside, but so giving and kind, especially to a kid like me who was so hungry for a bigger world, yet lost in my little one. Not only did she tutor me in chemistry; Gina also expanded my musical horizon, which up until then was decidedly dark and British. She made me special mixtapes of all her favorite albums and bootlegs from L.A. shows she was able to sneak into, mixes that prominently featured a messy and unpolished explosion of sound from Jane's Addiction, the Red Hot Chili Peppers, the Germs, and Thelonius Monster.

During the mid-to-late 1980s, L.A. was best known for its hair bands on the Sunset Strip (there was no shortage), but there were also super-cool sounds percolating on the fringes in tiny clubs throughout Hollywood, Santa Monica, and Pasadena. These incubators of punk, ska, psychedelic, and funk swirled together to make sounds I didn't think could work together, but somehow did. It was amazing, and once I knew about that sound, I couldn't stay away. I would hop in my little blue Civic, either solo or with a gaggle of friends, and head to Hollywood, eighty-five miles away, where I'd wrap myself with the sights and sounds like a warm, fuzzy bathrobe. My pal Tatum, a desert transplant by way of New York City, always knew about obscure clubs, record stores, pop-up shops and art shows. In our pre-internet world, I don't know how Tatum came about his knowledge, but he could always direct me to a fashion show out of a young designer's garage or the best pop-up vintage store so that I could source tailored 1940s jackets for my collection.

On one of these adventures, we found ourselves at a tiny makeshift gallery housed in a backyard not too far off Melrose and Fairfax. A sign on the fence instructed us to let ourselves in and we followed the sound of horns and percussion down a short path flanked with California poppies, up a stairwell leading to a loft space above a garage, only to be greeted by the kindest crowd and a roomful of large mixed-media sculptures and paintings. I remember little of the art now other than being moved by the boldness of color. What struck me most were the people, slightly older than us, unafraid to take up space. They didn't cower in false humility like my mom's church crowd or pander for attention like the hangers-on at the junkyard. They had work they wanted to share and so they did. They invited friends who invited friends who invited more friends. Anyone who came through that little gate down that flower-flanked path must be a friend, so they were welcome. The show was organized by Perry Farrell of Jane's Addiction and his then-girlfriend, artist Casey Niccoli. Again, how did Tatum know? I don't remember if Farrell and Niccoli were there during our visit, but I like to imagine they were among the exuberant circle holding court, handing out cheap champagne in Solo cups.

Until that point, I had only seen grown-up life modeled in very limiting ways. So to see adults have fun, make music and art, and hype one another up filled me to the brim with hope. Maybe I could do that, too. How does one pursue who and what they are? What are the rules—to follow or break? How to adapt… or not, and at what cost? The magic was in the "how." The seed of what was possible was sown. I just needed to figure out how I would continue my upward growth.

The more I drove, the more I hated to sit still. My focus in school, when I made it there, diminished completely. Afternoons and weekends at the junkyard were excruciating. I could not bring myself to sit at my barstool waiting for the phone to ring or the thick metal door to swing open. I had two strategies. One: wander into the yard as if in pursuit of some part. If I looked busy, no one would question the rambling. Two: monitor the junkyard hotline. This hotline connected over a hundred junkyards throughout the deserts, Inland Empire, and L.A. County. If you needed something, you simply picked up the receiver and announced what you were looking for and someone, somewhere, would answer if they had the part. For example:

"This is Robyn at B&R—I'm looking for a left fender for a 1981 Cadillac Eldorado. Needs to be super clean… it's for a body shop. Will travel to pick it up."

And with that, other countermen across the land would rush to answer as if it was the greatest of competitions. Whoever came in second or third would call directly, hoping to outbid whoever "won" on the hotline. They were also curious about the young voice making the request and would go to great lengths to make THE best deal so that I might pick it up myself. We would volley our terms back and forth until I got exactly what I wanted, and then with my dad's blessing, I would hop in the yard truck for pickup. Time to drive! Thank god!

Out of the desert I would go, down the pass, and through the cities sprawling into one another across the 10 and 60 Freeways. Most of these junkyards were located in troubled, gang-run neighborhoods. Cruising through, I was met with mean, quizzical stares. What the hell is this young, well-manicured white girl wearing all black doing driving a big-ass pickup truck up in here? It got even weirder when I confidently parked, hopped out, and made my way into the office to greet my fellow counterman and continue the negotiation. I didn't make sense.

Maybe it was youth, but I never worried. I somehow felt incredibly safe. It was as if the mere act of driving all those miles—a teenage girl on a parts mission—set me so far apart from the norm that no one dared touch me. With time, I found myself a respected member of the extended junkyard community. I might have been young, but I was smart and fair. I negotiated hard and would refuse any part that didn't meet my quality standards. After all, the part was a ploy. My real goal was simply to drive with purpose for a few hours. I was already winning at my little game.

I didn't fool myself. The guys at the other junkyards were not real friends. I knew that. And yet, I often felt closer to those scrappy countermen than to my friends at school. I liked to hear their stories. Like the men who worked for my dad, who had fled other places looking for stability or fresh starts, finding acceptance in this mishmash world of bruised and battered castoffs. Many hailed from Korea and Mexico, while others found refuge from gang-ridden L.A. in more inland towns like Fontana, Ontario, and Pomona. They were a hopeful collective of mostly late-twenty-somethings, seeing junkyard life as an opportunity filled with endless treasures waiting to be found. Or at least, that's how I interpreted them and they, in return, seemed to like what I was reflecting back at them. The early jokes about me being jailbait gave way to a two-way street of kindness and support. As a result, I had a steady stream of new destinations to add to my driving repertoire as well as something else: the inside scoop on how modern business works, something I'd find useful in the years to come as I set up my own business ventures.

Car design was shifting rapidly by the end of the 1980s, becoming more plastic and electronic. Designed to have shorter lives, vehicles and their inner workings were completely expendable compared to the boat-like metal vessels of the past. My dad railed against the constant change, refusing to stock more modern cars. He had four acres filled to the brim with pre-1980 vintages, dripping with usable parts, and yet his sales paled in comparison to the junkyards I visited, who had a fraction of land in which to house inventory.

Because of the lack of space, they had to be selective, scouring auction sales for the latest models, only to quickly strip off the usable parts to be warehoused, and send the rest along to scrap yards in Long Beach. These junkyards, housed in some of the diciest of neighborhoods, were a marvel of thoughtful design and process. I suppose it was strange for a girl to ask for guided tours, but I couldn't help myself. I wanted to know how others did this junkyard thing. I wanted to know what worked because clearly, my dad did not have this nailed down and my mom was becoming a hand-wringing pacing machine, never certain if all the bills could be paid from month to month.

No matter the junkyard, the guys were always overjoyed to stop everything and show me around, answering all my questions about inventory, vendors, timing, and roles; recycling versus scrapping; dogs versus security systems; computer communications versus phones. This business could be something bigger, I thought to myself, tickled with inspiration on my journey home. We had so much land and possibility. Picture it! Oil slicks, begone! Stacks of old Chryslers, off with your heads! Rows of racks clutching only the hottest parts in demand, inventoried and entered into a computer rather than our personal memory banks. Customers would flock to our desert outpost from the far reaches of Southern California. Why? BECAUSE WE WOULD HAVE IT ALL. And with it all, we would have money, money that might send me to college. My school friends already knew what was coming next: Stanford, USC, UCLA, UC Riverside, UC Irvine… all the UCs. It's what we AP students did (even us kids who ditched). We collected college brochures and dreamt of where graduation would take us.

This empire of riches in my mind would grow and grow as I pushed myself around the freeway back home, hip-checking my way into the fast lane in the big truck. With KROQ blasting through the speakers, I bobbed my head to the latest post-punk and alternative music that I knew about through Skinhead Gina and my *Rolling Stone* subscription. *Hear me!* the world seemed to proclaim. Craftsman bungalows and red-tiled mission-style homes dotted the communities off the freeway—big porches and archways, heavy doors, and manicured yards. I could picture future, mature me pulling into one of the houses—an old, boxy Volvo 240 in yellow swinging into the driveway like a boss. My house would have a giant fireplace flanked with bookshelves brimming with rare finds. A record player would take the place of a television; my vinyl collection alphabetized and extended up an entire wall. *See me! You want this*, said world.

Oh, yes. I do! I want that, too!

As the 10 Freeway inched east toward the 15 Freeway home, the houses became newer and less unique. Strip malls seemed to breed with wild abandon. KROQ was out of range and now a staticky connection of the past. Greenery gave way to yucca trees, and neither the junkyard empire life nor the cozy yellow Volvo craftsman one seemed within reach. I could feel the sparks of inspiration flutter away. No sound. No vision. Only the image of returning to my dad, scissor-kicking his blue-uniformed legs up and down the junkyard aisles. And my mom, with her stacks of unpaid bills. "I'm a nervous wreck," she would say to anyone, to no one, wringing hands, wringing dish towels, ringing true.

I settled into the divet of the bench seat, tapping my fingers on the gear shift, as if it could shift me into a new gear, too. Just me and the truck, filled with parts, traveling up the windy Cajon Pass, the future on hold.

Chapter 12
Fury

The Plymouth Fury was the descendent of an automobile dynasty. Produced by Plymouth beginning in 1955, the Fury one-upped its older sister, the Belvedere, with more rear fin, bells, and whistles, and then led a long life fluctuating between a full-size and mid-size rig as auto aesthetic trends dictated. The Fury line would eventually die of irrelevance on the Kenosha, Wisconsin plant line in 1988, but not before it would go through seven official generations—the most important one, according to my best friend, Greg Toliver, being the Fury III.

It should be noted that I disagree.

But before we discuss the merits—or lack thereof—of the Fury III, let us first discuss that my junkyard life was not something that I shared with many people. Not just anyone was allowed into that world of mine. I had learned to be a compartmentalizer early on out of necessity. This life strategy began in 5th grade when I finally met a cool girl—let's call her Beth—who I thought could be my friend. Not that she could ever replace Colleen, my best friend from my life before, but this new friend liked to laugh, dance to Duran Duran and Cyndi Lauper like I did, and she had a distinct fashion sense. All boxes checked.

But when Beth's parents learned about what my parents did, they were less enthused about our friendship. There was a phone interview with my mom, followed by several drive-bys on our house and business to determine if we were dirty, shady, and/or alcoholics, which was then followed by a cooling-off period to determine if we were really meant to be friends. My pride could barely stand it. I was from a place, a better one, where there were actually sidewalks. My parents were kind and generous and not dirty criminals. My mom even taught second grade catechism at Holy Family Catholic Church and had the rosary beads to prove it. She made sure our house was spotless, even the windows, and dinner was always ready at six. How dare Beth's parents think I wasn't friend-worthy. But, I did what any lonely kid would do: I swallowed my pride and focused all my energy on being an even better Robyn—an even better dresser, dancer, singer, soccer player, roller skater, bike rider, student, swimmer, sister, daughter, and friend. You name it, I made it my life's ambition to be better at it. After several weeks of scrutiny at soccer practice and at school with regular reports from my teacher to Beth's parents, my perfection was undeniable (and probably very boring). I won. Friendship was granted. However, I understood the cost: that miserable festering fury of being considered *less than* and pandering to course correct. I might have won the friendship for now, but I hated how I got there and I vowed it would never happen again. And so my strategy was devised: never talk about the family business. And for years, I didn't.

○ × ○

Given my strict rules and tried-and-true methods, I didn't know how I let my guard down. But one day in ninth grade, it happened: Greg Toliver weaseled his way into my heart, and by eleventh grade, into the junkyard. Greg had been my pal since our freshman year in P.E. when the fate of the alphabet had his 'T' follow my 'S' in the last name lineup.

We both loved skate culture, and he would often steal my high tops during class, leaving me to do jumping jacks in my socks. My high tops were imprinted with multi-colored pencils and were much cooler than his blue Vans, so I understood his motivation. I would often have to chase him into the boys' locker room to retrieve my shoes, turning my head to avoid the naked shower boys and tackling him to get my pencils back. It was a lot of work being his friend, but he made me laugh like no other with his Dana Carvey impersonations and random notes left in my notebook, like this:

My name is Greg.

I like daisies, slow walks on the beach, and choppin' broccoli.

I don't remember how he found out what my dad did. Perhaps he saw my dad drop me off in the tow truck before I had my own car and put the details together. I vaguely alluded to having an after-school and weekend job, leaving out the details so that I could stick to my code of privacy. I just remember that one day we went from a quick after-school reset of skateboarding (the Tolivers had a ramp in their backyard), eating manicotti (his mom always had a batch of cheesy manicotti in the fridge), and drinking Dr. Pepper, to a trip over to the junkyard so I could begin my shift. Greg's bulky blue El Camino trailed my petite blue Honda. Zigging and zagging in the most indirect way at top speeds, we cut through soft bluffs of desert until we hit the main roads, where a more dignified approach was expected. As if in a cool down, we pulled up to the hulking gates at a slow trot. I thought he would just turn around and go find other buddies to have an afternoon skate adventure. Instead, he turned his car off too and followed me inside.

Oh no. Oh no. My heart began to pound. Everything in my body screamed, "Get him out of here." Before I could consider my options, my dad came rushing through the back door to answer the ringing phone, glaring at me for standing on the wrong side of the yellow counter and not answering it myself. I wasn't sure which dad we were going to get. He looked weary and stressed, his blue uniform coated with grease, scribble marks covering his left hand of notes taken from phone calls. My mom was already gone for the day and he was on his own to man the office until I got there—and I was late. Very late because the manicotti was so good that I helped myself to seconds and then thirds, and then we may have made out but just a little because I was not his girlfriend and was not supposed to be doing anything like that, and then we took the long way through the desert, where I stood before him on the wrong side of the counter. Me and a spindly, quirky-yet-handsome boy with a goofy smile plastered across his face. Oh no. Oh no. This was very bad.

I braced myself for the Harry Saunders explosion, my hands gripping the back of the barstool, my face tight and unsmiling in stubborn fight mode, legs slightly askew as if stabilizing a mountain. My dad finished up the call and slammed down the receiver. Should we run? We should run. That won't be weird. Greg will understand, right?

I was so deep in my fight-or-flight conundrum that I somehow missed that Greg had shifted his position. He was sitting down at the counter, making himself comfortable. My dad plopped down into his tall stool on the other side of the counter. And just like that, the two of them were shooting the shit and laughing about something dumb. I put my book bag down and headed to the shop fridge filled with beer and Dr. Pepper, took a breather, then returned with three Dr. Peppers.

Greg smiled broadly. "Guess what?"

I looked at him with curiosity. What now? Could this day get any weirder?

"I work here now!" he proclaimed and lifted his Dr. Pepper in a celebratory cheers.

Oh no. Oh no. But I feigned a smile and said something like, "Cool!"

And just like that, Greg became our first official license plate remover and destroyer. Quite a resume builder. For a terrible wage, something like $.50 a plate, his sole job was to roam the aisles and unscrew any license plates that the yard guys missed upon acquisition of the car. The yard guys hated taking the time to detach the plates, so there was actually a lot of work for Greg. Sometimes the bolts that held the plates in place were so rusted that it took multiple tools, levers, and brute strength to pry them free. It became clear quickly that this was a lot of work for $.50, but initially, it didn't matter. It was a slow time business-wise, so I was able to leave my post in the office and run the aisles with him. I felt strange having this commingling of my compartments and yet after the shock of it, soon I found myself looking forward to our afternoon antics. Plus, Greg—who was no stranger to difficult dads himself—had a way with my dad, which I loved. A little tease and banter went a long way for dads like ours, and for a short time, it was almost like having old Harry back—the one who found everything and everyone funny.

Once Greg started working there, we would spend many afternoons stopping by the Toliver house for a quick snack and then over to the junkyard for our respective shifts. Greg would grab his official tools: clipboard to record the car and respective license plate number, screwdrivers, ratchet, wrench for just-in-case moments of destruction, and the most important tool—not for his job, but for our fun making—the smelly yellow grease marker. These afternoons would often devolve into an elaborate game of hide-and-seek. And there was no shortage of hiding spots. My favorite was an old trash truck that had ladders in several places on the exterior, which allowed me to climb into the body with ease and clamber down into its inner cavity, where I'd hide under one of its many ledges. There was an enormous clay cobra discarded at the bottom, which on first take always looked real and scared both Greg and my brother, who would sometimes join in the fun. Using the grease markers, we would scrawl notes or simple drawings to each other across windshields, fenders, and hoods as clues to where we might be. The whole place was our gallery. My dad was less enthused by our masterpieces, but let it slide. I think he secretly enjoyed watching us be so stupid and free.

"Robz, look at this beauty." Greg pointed to his favorite car standing alone at the end of Aisle One, not yet smashed or stacked for space.

"Um. Where? I see no beauty," I responded, as I always did to that well-worn topic of conversation.

We had grown bored of the day's antics. At this point, Greg may have made a whopping total of $3.50. The afternoon wind was picking up, which often meant we needed to find cover to avoid getting hit by some projectile—the hoods being the worst offenders. They had a lot of surface area and would pick up speed quickly.

The car he pointed to was an off-white 1971 Plymouth Fury III four-door sedan, more monstrosity than vehicle.

To me, the exterior communicated confusion. Stretching wide and long, it seemed to ask: "Do I want to be a car or a boat?" as if deep in a personality crisis over its own form and function. It didn't have the crisp lines or shorter wheelbase of the mid-1960s version, nor did it have the muscle car groove so popular in other lines, like the Chevy Nova.

"It's totally the best car in this whole shit pen," Greg insisted. "You gotta admit it."

I would do no such thing. Plus, our yard was not a shit pen.

I looked at the car again. It was bulbous and lacked decorum no matter what Plymouth had said back in the day: "Four hundred and forty four-barrel V-eight engine, AM and FM radio, seats six adults and sports nineteen-point-seven cubic feet of trunk. Fury is more car all around where you need it most." True, it was more car all around, and yet—who needed a trunk that could fit an entire football team? I couldn't get behind this aesthetic even for irony's sake. With an eye roll, I left Greg alone in the dust storm and sauntered off, back to my perch in the office, where I would pretend to be important, answering the few calls that came in or hopping on the wrecking yard hotline to simply connect to someone, anyone.

I needed to be important because 1) Greg had a new girlfriend who was not me, and 2) I was beginning to slip into something that felt very wrong. A bend in position here, a white lie there. I was shifting to be more liked (and hopefully loved), and also trying to be more *like*

Greg. He was clever and confident, or so I thought, and I wanted a slice of that for myself, because at that moment I was anything but. It was deeply uncomfortable to be witnessed as inept and weird by someone I loved so profoundly. And that was exactly why my worlds were not supposed to overlap. That was why there were rules. Why did I abandon my rules? And there I was, in poser-ville again, much like I felt when I first started at the junkyard. Only by that time, in addition to my unbearable pretense, my dad's temper was always lurking at a simmer, waiting to find a target in which to reach full boil. It was increasingly difficult to breathe, think, or talk. My heart spent its time racing, while my mind and tongue often went mute.

Greg and I would come back to that same tired car and aesthetic argument again and again. The further time went on, the more we both dug in our heels. We would have gladly died on the sword for our points of view. Looking back, I understand that it was the one topic that—although inconsequential—was one of the only exchanges that could be loud and truthful. I wasn't the only one bending and white-lying, even though it felt like it at the time. Everyone around me, including Greg, was trying on new personas, struggling to find what lit them up amidst our bleak desert setting. We were all pushing through what needed to be endured and what, cathartically, needed to be discarded. Who and what were we supposed to be? Our families had vague ideas. Our culture offered a variety of options. School and church had some strong suggestions as well. But what do you do when everything feels uncomfortable, like a scratchy wool sweater?

~ × ~

One afternoon Greg and I arrived a few moments apart to find Harry on a rampage. I don't remember what set off the temper tantrum now, but we arrived to find my dad ripping around the office yelling incomprehensible gibberish, kicking whatever was in his path. Luckily my mom was already gone for the day, because this was a much worse explosion than the usual *so-and-so did me wrong* kind of anger. These moments were tricky. Sometimes, I could inject some light teasing to shake his anger free. Other times, it was best to be silent and let the tantrum run its course.

This is not about me. This is not about me. This is not about me. He is angry. This is his anger. This is not your anger... I would repeat this on the inside, a well-worn refrain since as long as I could remember, trying to create a barrier between him and me so I would not be scared. He continued to yell and kick. Without making eye contact, Greg grabbed his keys, and with an "I'm outta here," he took off. I didn't know at that moment but it would be Greg's last day at the junkyard. My chest tightened in shame. Finally, Greg had seen enough. My dad was weird. I was weird. Together, we were unbearable people not even worthy of a goodbye. In retrospect, this departure was long overdue—the job was not exactly a money-maker on his part, and the boredom was a heavy weight. My dad's tantrum was a good excuse to jump ship. I ran after Greg, but he peeled out of the parking lot without looking back.

Back in the office, my internal mantra changed its tune. *This is not about me* became a chorus of *me me me me me*. I am angry. I am angry. I am angry. AT YOU. My dad was still tossing things around. I stomped toward him with a rage to match his own.

"KNOCK IT OFF!" It rumbled and tumbled out with ferocity, a new sensation to my body. I couldn't remember the last time my voice had picked up speed and volume. And there was my hand. Moving. Upward. Making contact. With his face. Oh no. I just hit my dad. I could feel the prickly stubble of his cheek in the palm of my hand. He was silent now but staring at me with a hatred I had never seen before. I hurt him and the door in his heart was closing with me on the outside.

Without another word, I grabbed my keys and stormed out. I would drive for hours that afternoon and early evening, alternating between tears and more anger. I did wrong and I knew it. But there was something else brewing inside me. Was it pride? After years of watching and enduring my dad's bad behavior, this was my moment. It wasn't the invisible variety of bad—lying, posturing, or stealing. It wasn't like that time I lied about spending the night at Jennifer's when I was really in Hollywood for the night vintage store shopping and listening to music. Or, that time I lied to Greg's brother about smoking weed to seem more experienced (self-preservation) so that I didn't have to indulge as the pipe was passed around (I was terrified of drugs. If I said I already did it, that meant no one would force my hand). No. This was blatant and true. I was angry and made myself felt and heard. And, I was not sorry. I was caught in the act of being very bad. How ugly. How wrong, but somehow very right. It was time to own it and grow.

A few weeks later, I ran into Greg after school, skating in a parking lot. We had been avoiding one another at school and no longer called each other at night while we ate Pop-Tarts and dished the dirt on our respective days. Long gone were the nights of driving out to the edges of the desert, looking at stars and listening to Pink Floyd in his El Camino. Long gone were the days of fingers grasping for one another, a secret when friends weren't looking. In teenage time, a day is a lifetime, so at that point, we were several lifetimes away from one another. I was trying out a new look that day, something not all-black. In fact, it was a white button-down shirt and a light-wash jean, the opposite of my usual thrifted dark palette.

"Hey, you look pretty. You *should* do more of that," he offered after saying hi. What I would have given to hear those words just three weeks before. Pretty. Me. I looked down at my bland vanilla ensemble and all I could hear was *should should should should. You should do more of that.*

Wait. A. Second.

No. I should not. I will not.

I am not a Plymouth Fury III. That's why I hated the car so much. It was trying too hard with its hideous bulbous side panels, AM/FM radio, and V8 motor to power over the highways and appeal to the masses. It should be fast. It should be sporty. It should not be able to fit another car in its trunk.

I should be a good daughter. I should be a good student. I should be a pretty girl. I should grin and bear my dad's temper tantrums. I should ask for forgiveness. I should know more about cars. I should not complain. I should wear normal clothes. I should be more experienced in the way of sex and drugs. I should be more demure—no, less demure. I should have my future figured out. I should go to UC Berkeley, or maybe Stanford. I should have parents that understand this. I should be loyal (but to whom?). The list of shoulds could go on forever. Maybe I was some of those things *sometimes*, but there was a cost to all this shoulding. In all my striving, I had been trying too hard and I had lost track of the only should that mattered: I should tell the truth. To myself. I did not need to do anything more than to ask myself, is this true to me? If yes, proceed. There may be consequences. Own them. If no, find another way. There may also be consequences. Own them. I did not need to do anything more than just be me. And this me really really really wanted to go home and light these dumb clothes on fire. And just like that, the spell of Greg was gone. I slowly smiled, feeling so free. With a quick "Bye" I turned away and walked toward my car.

A few days later, armed with a yellow grease marker in hand, I made my way to the Fury on Aisle One and marked "Greg was here" across the windshield, an homage to my friend and his rejection—the rejection that ironically taught me to love all my compartments no matter how nutty they might be.

"Okay, Mo." I motioned to Mo in the forklift. "Let's get it out of here."

⸎ ✕ ⸏

Several years later, when I was roughly twenty-four, I hopped in a friend's car at Scripps College in Claremont, California. Gina was a talented ceramics student only a couple years younger than me. Somehow I had been gifted the opportunity to manage the Ruth Chandler Williamson Gallery on campus, where I was responsible for hanging shows and tending to the vast collection of ceramics alongside someone who would change my life forever, my mentor Kirk Delman (more on him later). Gina was one of my first friends post-college, who made me feel like being creative and making art weren't completely impractical pursuits.

Gina and I had spent the day in the gallery getting ready for the annual senior show, painting walls and discussing what stories the various works were trying to share with us. The students were ambitious and often wanted to erect large structures, but very few knew how to use tools. That was where my junkyard resume came in handy. I wasn't always skillful, but I wasn't afraid to grab a power tool and get a little dirty. It had been an exhilarating day of thinking and doing and then it was time to step away to celebrate at The Press, a favorite Claremont restaurant where the food was always sourced locally and the music was carefully curated.

I grabbed the door handle of Gina's beefy blue car and out wafted the scent of beach artifacts from her home in the San Francisco area—lining her dash was driftwood encased in salt water, shells, dried flowers. I smiled immediately. It was so uniquely Gina and a breath of fresh air compared to the BMWs, Mercedes, and other pedigreed cars belonging to the Scripps girls. "It used to be an undercover police car in Philly," she explained with pride as we pulled out of the parking lot and headed to the restaurant. I knew that car. I knew that car well. "Plymouth Fury, right, Gina?"

She smiled at me in that *You are my person, I am your person way* and gushed, "*Gran* Fury."

☙ ✕ ❧

Thirty-five years later, I will call Greg. I want to know how his life has turned out. But that's a half-truth; a soundbyte to gain entry. I want to tell him all of this, waiting for a pause between his story and mine. But even all these years later, I cannot say it aloud. So I write it here.

Alright Greg, I concede. You were right, she's a beauty. I see it now.

Chapter 13
Supper

"Count to five, turn it. Count to five, serve it."

A round of fake laughs.

We were at the diner owned by Nick the Greek across the railroad tracks. We went there often. So often, that the waitress would write down my dad's liver and onions order before we even sat down in our brown pleather booth. She was kind to him even though he was dirty and rude (although he thought he was funny). Harry liked to "razz" people, especially waitresses. He had convinced himself that they liked it.

As I moved through my teenage years, I was old enough to see their eyes tighten every time he opened his mouth. I could also see other diners stare at him as he grunted and lapped up his dinner like a wild animal. He ordered liver and onions because it was a meal he remembered from his childhood. He did not order other dishes because he could not read the menu and would not let us read to him in public. At the end of every meal, he would declare that he loved food. No one who loves food would treat a meal like this—inhaling raw liver and onions and allowing it to dribble down his chin, finally resting in a pool on his growing belly. Once starved, never full. He never seemed to taste or enjoy anything.

I was not embarrassed by him. I had too much compassion for where he came from and for how hard he worked during the day. And yet as I grew older, I started to feel something new. A distinction between us. An annoyance for his lack of dignity. He taught me to be ambitious and yet there he was eating like the lowest common denominator, with dirty hands that never wash clean.

⸺ ✕ ⸻

I was not who I thought I was.

The world was not what I thought it was.

The nightly news would report tragedy: the nuclear explosion at Chernobyl, the disintegration of the Space Shuttle Challenger, the devastation of AIDS. Settled deep into the brown recliner in the family room, the six o'clock news would stir and shock me. Why was everyone and everything dying?

The Sunday *Los Angeles Times* would report hope—weekly redemption from the nightly news cycle: the dismantling of the Berlin Wall, the creation of a new-fangled information source called the Internet, the Cure was scheduled for a show at Dodger Stadium (must make money for tickets; must design a new skirt).

My *Rolling Stone* subscription would spark inspiration: the shapeshifting of David Bowie, the soul-searching of U2, the sexuality of Madonna, the new psychedelic sounds of the Stone Roses and the Manchester scene.

The daily grind at school would reveal kindness and purpose: the gifts of literature, art, and friendship from the most unlikely kids and teachers. I would begin allowing school friends into my home, my mom ordering pizza for us as we worked through the night writing plays, discussing books, and listening to music on my new CD player. These friends would take the place of my brother, our age gap too wide now, our interests too different. Ryan and my mom would spend every morning screaming at one another, always at war about going to school, eating breakfast, brushing teeth, changing clothes. He and I would go for days without speaking. There was no point in engaging him.

And the junkyard. Well, it too would continue to reveal itself, churning through people and machines with little regard. Perhaps it was less about revelation, but more about our own acceptance that nothing was meant to survive in the walled fortress. It was impossible to coexist with an orchestra of death—forklifts stabbing windshields, bulldozer lifts crumpling cars into bite-sized pieces, impact drills roaring and dissecting engine cores—and not be completely humbled by the power of destruction.

My place in the center of that world was becoming more defined, working its way into a larger association of connections: a web of other wrecking yards, repair shops, and police—all extending a giant net to catch me as I hurled myself toward adulthood. I had a lot of firsts centered around that junkyard. My first car was put together by a group of guys at other wrecking yards; my first ticket ripped up by the cop I sold a transmission to the day before; my first car accident repaired by the body shop down the street without a word to my dad. To most, I was a sweet novelty act to be cherished. This was a lucky reception that I understood and was grateful for, even at the time. It helped me remember my value when older men would go too far, grazing a breast with grubby hands or threatening to hurt me if I didn't give them parts for free. Or worse, speaking to me as if I was weak. I was young, yes, but never weak.

Although I was becoming more open to friends spending time in my room and speaking truths deep into the night, the junkyard world—especially after the Greg fiasco—continued to be private. Very few of my school friends knew what my dad did for work or how I spent my time away from school. To his credit, Harry steered clear of the nightly meetings in my room, never once trying to kick in the closed door like he used to do when I was little. These two worlds—his and mine—remained separate from one another.

It was not that I was ashamed, exactly, but I didn't know how to explain.

I liked feeling isolated, just me and my dad taking on the world.

I thought we were invincible.

I hated feeling isolated, just me and my dad taking on the world.

We were not invincible.

⸺ × ⸺

At a certain point, there's a natural rift that occurs between parent and child; child and world. It fissures every which way, rumbling and tumbling in San Andreas fault proportions. Little breaks yield chasms and before you know it, you're standing on your very own tectonic plate, ducking and covering in preparation for the next aftershock. Without precedent or vocabulary, it's terrifying to feel so alone. Now, as a mother to a teenager, I understand the change—the shift between cute and dependent, to fierce and independent. With age and experience, I cherish these developments in my own daughter—her edges becoming more defined, her center holding without me. My parents, my father in particular, were not prepared for my seismic shifts in mood, appearance, or interests. How could they be? The world that they thought they knew was marching on without them and that world included me.

By my late teens, the tension between my dad and I had been building for some time. I tried to brush it off, often pretending that it was just a bad day or bad week. My dad and I didn't see eye to eye, or I was annoying to my mom again, or vice versa. But the truth was that our tension was not temporary. It was a deeper, more permanent crack in our foundation. For me, it came to a head in the form of a cat. Five cats to be exact. I was roughly seventeen years old when I found them in an old Ford pickup on Aisle Two. Little kitten meows escaped from the driver's window and drew me in. I grabbed the handle and pulled the rusty door off its hinges. There on the sun-cracked seat were five kittens, side by side.

Excited, I grabbed one, only to find it was attached at the torso to its brother, who was attached to the next sibling at the belly as well. They were conjoined, four alive with a dead one on the end. I swooped them off the seat and carried them in my shirt to the office. I examined them closely, noticing the extra wrinkle of skin where they were attached. Grabbing some matches, peroxide, and a sharp knife, I planned to detach them and make them whole. Nobody questioned me as I called a vet to see if this could be done. Nobody questioned me as I began cutting the dead kitten from the live ones. The meows increased to screeches and blood streamed down my barely-sanitized knife. Tears flooded my face as I tried to hold the skin together to stop the insides of the limp kitten from pouring out. I couldn't fix them. My dad finally stepped in, immune to my tears, and told me to kill them. A small mercy, but how?

My lips swelled from the salty tears, preventing all words.

I wish I could tell you that I argued.

I wish I could tell you I bundled the kittens, drove to the vet, and saved the day.

I said nothing.

I did what I was told. I followed Harry's orders before he marched off toward whatever he was doing, leaving me to deal with it on my own.

A pail was filled with water.

The cats inserted.

They did not sink.

They kept floating, tiny screaming heads trying to stay above the water line.

Please die. Please. Please. Please.

I cradled their tiny gray heads.

I'm so sorry. I'm so sorry. I'm so sorry.

I placed a shop towel over the pail.

I can't, I whispered through my sobs to Aaron, one of the yard guys trying to walk away from my mess.

I can't, I whispered again. Aaron nodded as I walked away, leaving my mess to him.

This is the event I remember, the moment when everything changed. I couldn't reconcile my lack of knowledge nor that of my father's. I had lost track of why we opened our doors every morning; why we ran through the desert heat searching for a part that may or not work for the desperate customer at the counter. Or maybe, I never understood what we were doing to begin with.

Did it ever have a purpose?

Could he see past his survival? Could he see a future for me? Could he see me?

Connected to him, I was one of those kittens, but there was no one to cut me free.

⌒ ✕ ⌒

And so the late 1980s marched on. Cars became more complicated, my dad's hanger-on groupies became drunker, the industry became more computerized, and with that, the needs of customers became less reliant on used parts. Advances in automation within manufacturing meant that aftermarket parts and accessories were becoming cheaper to make and easier to source. Why buy a used part, freshly washed in the Safety Kleen chemical bath by a young girl, when you could simply buy a brand new one for the same price or better? With each passing year, availability and ease increased for new parts and new cars, and with that, business fizzled up to dribs and drabs, leaving my dad even more frustrated and angry. His temper accompanied him everywhere; a seemingly calm exchange of small talk at the gas station could escalate into a storm of racial slurs without provocation. If I arrived a few minutes late for work from school, I would be greeted by a slammed door and curse words. It often made more sense to ditch work than to endure the wrath of Harry. But all of this paled in comparison to dinner time.

In a restaurant, we feigned good manners. At home was an entirely different story. Enter the table, four chairs, placemats, cutlery, salad, his blue cheese salad dressing next to his plate. Enter my mom, quickly trying to put something together because *he* was home and *he* was hungry. Enter me and Ryan sliding into our spots, tired after a day of school and bracing ourselves for what might come at that night's dinner table.

I can see it like it's happening. Still in his dirty blue uniform, dad plops into his chair, his bloated belly brushing against the table. He begins stabbing his fork at food before my mom even sits down at the table, grunting with each inhale. He does not look at us. Stab, grunt, swallow. Repeat. Sometimes he chokes and the three of us look at one another, silently communicating, What do you think? Heimlich? Or will it pass?

He gasps for air and just as one of us is about to intervene, we are greeted with a projectile and a high-pitched cursing. Choking or not, he will scrape every last scrap off his plate and then dip into seconds, usually before the rest of us have buttered our bread. Once he's shoved enough in, that's when he lifts up his head and takes us in as if noticing for the first time that we, too, are at the table. By that point, Ryan or I have said something dumb, like: "Too bad we don't have any chocolate ice cream." Or my mom asks a too-specific work question, like: "Did you end up selling that transmission today?"

And just like that, down with the fork.

His steel-toed boots kick his chair back. His club hands grab the lip of the table. Up, up, up the table goes. Down, down, down the plates and dinner descend, clanking to the floor, scattering to the far corners of the dining room. The grunt is replaced with a high-pitched squeal: "I might as well just kill myself!"

Does he mean it? We never know. Maybe today is the day he's had too much. He stomps off to his barn in the backyard. My mom sighs and the three of us clean up the mess without further discussion, then retreat to our various corners of the house, listening for if and when he returns.

I remember after one of the first table flips, I shared what had happened with a teacher at school. We had an assignment to do a ten minute free write about how we spent the prior evening. Still shaky from my dad's storm, I quickly recapped dinner and the subsequent outburst. The truth was that I was worried about us. Do dads often yell that they are going to kill themselves? Is that a thing? What happened to the dad that used to pick me up from school dances and patiently listen to all the details over a celebratory 7-Eleven hot dog? Or the dad who rushed to the school parking lot when I needed my battery jumped, not raising a question or a single eyebrow over my obvious attempt to ditch school? My body felt heavy, flooded with sadness. I needed help and I didn't know how to ask my friends. I also didn't want them to know that home was less than perfect. So, I turned in my free write, a scribbled plea, and waited.

The next day, my paper was returned with a note and an F: *This is not appropriate. You are not this type of kid.* What type of kid was I, then? Did my teacher think I was making it up? He thinks I am a liar. Oh no. Oh no. I am a liar. He thinks I am a terrible person. I am so tired. My eyes closed. I could feel tears welling and my face running hot. My teacher began the day's lecture, his baritone voice droning on without meaning. What type of kid was I? He only saw my parents showing up for parent/teacher night—on time and friendly in nice clothing. They were proud of me and said as much. How dare I speak poorly of them? How dare I share that my dad was struggling and suicidal? How dare I.

What kind of kid was I? There wasn't a clear answer, but now I knew: this was to be filed away in the silent pile. And I should avoid dinner at all costs, even if it meant going hungry.

My mom, who had been quietly picking up the pieces behind the scenes, paying the bills and praying for us, stepped out from the shadows. She had established a DMV service when they first bought the junkyard, a side hustle for helping car collectors navigate the complexity of getting clean titles for their vintage finds. Out of necessity, this side hustle became the real hustle, which only made my dad more temperamental. But Karen Saunders was not about to lose her home because of her husband's weird junkyard dream gone wrong.

Looking back now with full understanding of the years of war and grief still ahead of her, I don't know how she hung on. Maybe that's the true divide between us. Marriage, according to her Catholic beliefs, wasn't up for negotiation. Pray, and guidance will be provided. Suffer, and martyrdom will gain you access to heaven. There was no quitting in her mind, but I often wonder what her life would have been like had she bailed. What if she was able to surround herself with beauty and joy far, far away? What if she was able to sleep through the night without worry? None of us knew it yet, but life was about to get worse for her before it would get better. The storm was coming.

⌒ ✕ ⌒

My dad's groupies, the hangers-on who loved to hold court on the barstools and raid the fridge for beer, would soon be traded out for something darker. Meth, which had been a whisper for years, had become a roar. It was everywhere—even in my high school cafeteria, the stoner kids complementing their nachos with shared bumps from little blue spoons. We would hear about labs scattered all over and under the desert run by tweakers, homespun scientists, and more often than not—according to the papers—Mexican cartels. The vast high desert provided seemingly-unlimited spaces to whip up chemical concoctions of varying purity and expertise without detection. And with this, we started to see a new batch of people at the junkyard. It was quickly becoming a haven for a desperate crowd who stripped down cars for any metals and copper wire that could be quickly cashed in at the scrap yard down the street to fund their habits.

My dad, erratic and a little crazy himself by that point, didn't understand the new groupies but couldn't get rid of them. They crept in during the day and moved into vans on the property. Unbathed hungry ghosts roaming the aisles. Emaciated and toothless, they took everything: parts, tools, my dad's reputation, any remaining customers, and finally, my brother.

It wasn't obvious at first. Ryan was twelve or thirteen, too young for it to be true. The shifts were subtle. His clothes loosened and then needed a belt. His blue eyes hardened into opaque marbles, his cheeks grew sunken and pockmarked. He frequented an old Dodge van at the end of Aisle One several times a day. Old friends were discarded. Ryan will tell you now that he has no regrets. If he had a chance to do it again, he would not make changes. I'm not sure this is true, but I allow him these musings.

Merely a tween, my little brother became cruel and erratic. His voice began to change, not just from puberty but from the twitchiness. A fast clip that slurred and made no sense. He did not graduate from high school and instead nested in our parents' house, stealing anything that could be pawned. He continued to age without growing up, cycling through friends and girlfriends, losing teeth and breaking bones in fights. Many tried to step in, to talk reason. Addicts love to talk; they do not love reason. He did not get help. He broke hearts and windows. One day, I found a red ceramic tile covered in crystaled residue in the garage—out in the open—and knew that I had lost him forever.

The ache and tears of loss were so overpowering that I didn't hear the police cars the night they chased me down the highway, the night I sped far, far away from him and the darkness he represented. "Officers, I'm sorry. My brother is dead," I told them as they put their guns away and wrote me a ticket instead. Ryan was twenty the day he left us a note saying he wanted to die. He was found, his body alive but his spirit gone.

The cycle kept going. Drugs, guns, more fights. Jail time. He continued to age and eventually got clean-ish and a job. A son was born. The family thought, This may be it! We rejoiced over the little blue-eyed blond boy, filled with hope that a normal, easier life might be in reach. A few more years went by on the edge of almost—almost okay. But a few years later, Ryan's partner would die and he would start the process again. My parents kept him close, forever hopeful, remarking on how he loved to polish odd chunks of metal and keep the garage clean. They marveled at his skill while I raised his beautiful son.

But that is getting too far ahead in this story. Ryan cares for my parents when I cannot. At some point along the way, we traded seats at the table.

Chapter 14
Rosary Beads and Roller Skates

In the late 1970s and early eighties, weekend roller skating got us through the school week. We would obsess about our outfits, shoelaces, and the pizzazz we would add to the Hokey Pokey. This was the one place where we could be extra and no one would judge us—a huge gift for us Catholic kids. We could move our bodies and sing to racy lyrics. Our skate skirts were short to intentionally show off our limbs, made powerful by our soccer, gymnastics, and skating repertoires. Yes, we were just kids, but we oozed strength and ambivalence to rules. The rink was not a place for the meek or the goody-goody—it was a place that fortified our autonomy.

And yet, from time to time, there would be a crossover of these worlds. I remember one of my earliest nights at the rink, back when I was only seven years old. The music had gone from a banger, Devo's "Whip It" ("Crack that whip [give the past a slip] Step on a crack [break your mama's back]" …Are we allowed to break Mama's back? That's a baddie; I like it.)—to my most behated moment of the night: the slow jam. Couples would join hands and float across the floor. I hated them and looked around, hoping that Stephen McGill would find me and want to link fingers for the ultimate dance of love under the lights. I thought by remaining on the floor, this might be the night. I inched away from the wall and prayed: "Dear God, I know that I am a bad kid and can't always be trusted, but I promise to be good if I could just skate with someone tonight." I skated a few more feet forward, enshrouded in the darkness reserved for slow, romantical songs.

And then it happened. I felt the smooth grasp of boy hands. BOY HANDS. I was linked with another. A BOY! Could it be Stephen McGill? Was he drawn to my spark from across the rink? We rounded the corner, still linked. A strobe light illuminated our union. Perhaps it was karma for my blasphemous request, but instead of Stephen McGill's gentle face and soft curls, I found my fingers entwined with a handsome, bespectacled man with dark, slicked-back hair. Uh oh. I know who this is. I should have been more specific in my prayer. My eyes wandered downward, resting on the white clerical collar that could only belong to one person. Father Foley.

Bless me, Father, for I have sinned. It's been two weeks since my last confession. As we skated I recalled our last exchange, just a week ago in the dark confessional booth:

I socked my little brother every day this week.

I lied about how I got this scratch on my face (fighting with my friend's brother).

I had mean thoughts about Cheryl D. and I cut up her orange Brownie scarf in envy.

I stole a pinto bean from the store. I put it in my pocket without paying for it and then put it back. So technically, I didn't steal it, but I wanted to. I am a thief.

I coveted Alan's Clash cassette. Wait, I did more. I snuck into his room and listened to it when he wasn't home. I am a thief.

I was selfish. My dad works really hard, but it's not enough and I want better roller skates.

I'm a really bad person.

He knew. He knew I was a very bad person. In his strong Irish accent, he had given me a penance of ten Hail Marys, two Our Fathers, and suggested an apology to my brother was in order. I was not sorry for any of it, so only did one Hail Mary, no Our Fathers, and most certainly did not apologize to my bratty brother. And now here we were, hands clasped, bodies swaying together as Bill Withers crooned, "Ain't no sunshine when she's gone. It's not warm when she's away…" Father Foley knew a thing or two about skating, his feet scissoring around the corner with ease. I stopped looking for Stephen McGill and settled into our rhythm, our moves dazzling around the other couples, lights flickering across my body like stardust. In my seven short years on the planet, I might have been the biggest sinner, but I had never been more beautiful or talented. Just as the song ended, I bravely looked up at Father Foley's face and smiled. Years later, I would come across an article in the *Orange County*

Register about Father Foley and his fall from grace, like so many Catholic priests. But in that moment, he squeezed my hand with kindness, one sinner to another, and simply let me go.

Growing up Catholic meant that I had a long list of what was considered right and what was most certainly wrong. I used my rosary beads a few times a week, hoping that by rubbing each bead, I would rub my way closer to sainthood. More rubbing than praying, which was probably part of the problem. I was falling short all over the place. The idea of a higher power, or at least the concept that something bigger and benevolent was in charge, was important to me—oversight was needed. It was obvious that humans shouldn't be allowed to run completely free.

Although I loved the accoutrements of Catholicism—my white First Communion dress sewn lovingly by my mom, my vast collection of colorful rosary beads, and saint cards reflecting the humble heroics throughout the ages—the walls of the church and the contrived words of Sunday's homilies always felt as if they were closing in on me. No matter the church, I would often stand in line for Communion (mainly to show off whatever ensemble I had put together for the day—vanity was often on my confession list) and then as quickly as possible I'd place the Communion wafer on my tongue, make the sign of the cross, and hightail it out the door to find sun and air. I would not look back, as I did not want to see the shame register on my mom's face. It was bad enough that her husband did not attend church, and here I was embarrassing her in front of her fellow catechism teachers.

That stage left exit began early on and only became worse as I got older. I remember one time, just a few weeks short of my fifteenth birthday, I took a solo trip to Mississippi to visit my cousin, Tami. A couple of years my senior, she had become my pen pal and I could not wait to bask in the glow of this cool older cousin. Added benefit: it meant two whole weeks away from my duties at the junkyard. Tami knew things like all good older cousins do. Things like driving and boys and all the words to the latest Poison album. But before we would drive, tease our hair with Aquanet, kiss boys, sing "Every Rose Has Its Thorn," and sip moonshine from a spoon at the corner Sonic, we spent the first day of my trip in the French Quarter of New Orleans.

After inhaling beignets at Café Du Monde, drinking hurricanes from Pat O'Brien's, weaving our way through the narrow streets, and finding shelter from the humid heat under the terraced old buildings, we made our way, as all good Catholics would, to Saint Louis Cathedral. Whoosh. Four hands were required to push the heavy wood door inward. One step. Then another. Our right hands dipped holy water from the font on the wall and made signs of the cross with extra focus. Silent and forward we moved toward a pew. A wave of frankincense and myrrh assaulted my nose. I looked upward at the centuries-old vaulted ceiling. Red light filtered through the stained glass windows. There was no denying it. This was a beautiful place. "Look at how beautiful we are together," it seemed to say. "I want to believe in you, young sinner, but only if you believe in me."

The incense launched a full attack. Just as the beauty registered, my admiration was stopped in its tracks. I could not breathe. For a space of such epic proportions, it was closing in on me. I will not be judged by you, you stupid smelly building. You don't know me.

My heart began to race in that way. That way that has told me to flee since as long as I could remember. Without looking at my aunt or cousin, I stood up and scurried to the front door. With my full body weight, I yanked the door open, all the while holding my breath, defending my lungs from the incense and candle smoke.

Jackson Square in all its green vibrance stood before me. The humid air oddly offered a reprieve. Was it the hurricane from Pat O'Brien's for lunch, the cacophony of street musicians, the lushness of the square, or maybe the heavy sky threatening a downpour? The world was slushy and swirling around me. Whatever combination of elements, my heart found its pace and I heard a peaceful whisper in my heart: "Hey kiddo, I'm out here." Outside. I'm out here. I am not that, but this. God, Spirit, Source: call it what you will. In that moment, I found peace and it wasn't manmade.

Two weeks later I was back in California, back to the junkyard, back to Sunday Mass, and back to my very best avoidance tactics. Confirmation was looming, which meant I needed to attend Monday night teen classes.

Instead of God and commitment, I only found more rhetoric and a couple of bullies from school who pulled rank and spent the entire session making fun of everyone in the class. So, similar to Sundays, I would roll in to get my name checked off, then roll out to the bathroom and walk in the surrounding desert until it was time for my mom to pick me up.

Once I began driving myself, it became clear that Confirmation was not going to be a holy sacrament I would receive. Try as I might, I could not convince myself to steer out of my neighborhood, down 'I' Street, and make a left into Holy Family Church. Instead I used the time wisely—but with guilt—to drive and listen to music, mostly U2's "Unforgettable Fire." Its poetry seemed a vessel of divinity, and perhaps, a sufficient swap for whatever we were memorizing at Confirmation class. My allergic reaction to church was an honest one, but I didn't want to completely disappoint my mom, so I did my best to double down and figure out this God stuff on my own terms, reading the Old Testament and then the New and then the Old again, locking in on the Book of Ruth, Job, and the Song of Solomon as my favorites. I had heard excerpts my whole life at Sunday Mass—fragmented cheats plucked to prove some point or to provide an easy rote incantation. Reading passages in their entirety as literature rather than religious text was a luxurious effort. I wanted to hate it, but couldn't. The storytelling held up.

It was enough, those readings, to keep me going to Mass and remain connected to my mom. I could sit in the pew next to her piety sans my own and listen to the excerpts, recalling the larger stories I read late into the night. I could raise my voice in song, ignoring the irrational lyrics because it felt good to make sound and take up space.

The more I read from the Bible, the more I knew that whatever divinity was, it wasn't made special by the walls of a church. And the rules? What of the rules of how to live and be? The Ten Commandments were pretty clear about not coveting, stealing, making false idols, etc. All around me, adults and kids alike—but especially adults— were weaving in and out of the rules, bending under the weight of survival and self preservation. When money is scarce, holding fast to honor for the sake of principle leaves one hungry. I didn't understand the depth of these compromises until I stepped out on my own and into the lean years of college. At that moment, it was simply a confusing play to observe on an unstable stage. Even my mom would hang up her rosary beads and look the other way to keep up appearances and put food on the table and make the house payment. The junkyard was no longer a cash cow like it was in the early days, so principles were often downgraded to mere suggestions.

It was frustrating to watch the adults stumble all over the place when I needed them the most, but I took it as a sign that I needed to look elsewhere for some inspiration. Plus, I simply needed to lighten up and get on with having some fun before this high school gig was over. So, I turned the page and did what any teenage girl who is ready for the next chapter does: I cut all my hair off, repainted my room a vibrant gemstone green, bought the new Stone Roses and Deee-Lite albums, and infused some vintage hippie chic into my wardrobe. It was time for color and life and dancing. And just as my feet found a new groove in my senior year, enter a new friend: Peter.

A pattern was forming that has continued throughout my life. As I become ready and open to new perspectives, a new friend or experience drops into my life to help widen the view. Oddly, this one showed up in the venue voted least likely to expand horizons: my mom's church on a random Wednesday evening when I was in twelfth grade. Getting to church on Sunday took a lot of effort on my part, so the fact that I was in a pew next to my mom on a weekday evening after my junkyard shift was a pure miracle if there ever was one. And the place was packed to night club proportions. Folks came from all over in their Wednesday best to hear about recent apparitions of Our Lady of Medjugorje in the Bosnian countryside.

As the story goes, in 1981, Mary (mother to Jesus, yes, that Mary) appeared to six Croat teenagers. "A young woman about twenty years old," they said, "with blue eyes, black hair, and a crown of stars around Her head. She wore a white veil and bluish-gray robe." Each of the kids said they had not been able to see the Virgin's feet, and described Her as hovering just above the ground on a white cloud, as she spoke in a singing voice to them. The kids would continue to see her vision over the years, as would others as the story began to gain traction and

Medjugorje—although in the middle of political turmoil and religious conflict—became a pilgrimage site for many believers. The voice of the visiting priest, who recently made the pilgrimage and now seemed to be on a world tour, was mesmerizing, bellowing and then dropping to a whisper as if telling us a great secret. Colorful votive candles flickered on the other side of him, the overhead lights dim and gothic.

I shifted my weight, attempting to make myself comfortable on the hard wooden pew, crossing and uncrossing my legs, adjusting my vintage polyester plaid slacks that had a way of riding up and squeezing the life out of me. All this contorting broke the spell and I looked away from the priest, over to the block of pews running perpendicular to ours, locking eyes with a sandy-haired, bespectacled boy, who was openly smiling at me and my obvious pew discomfort. I smiled back, my heart kicking up a Motown double beat.

"Do you think the visions are real?" he asked, brushing cookie crumbs off his hands.

I took another bite of chocolate chip cookie, gaining a pause to think on it. As soon as the lecture was over, we had both beelined it to the reception hall in search of each other and the cookie score. Cookies in hand, I shyly introduced myself. There was something so warm and honest about him. Now that we were close up, I could tell he was several years older than me. Regardless, he needed to be my friend.

"I don't think it matters," I finally replied. "If it gives hope to some, then that's as real as it needs to be." We stood next to each other, arm to arm, immediately thick as thieves, observing the adults chattering, repeating the priest's stories as if we weren't all in the church together just a few short minutes ago. If any crowd needed hope, it was this one. There was something so perpetually lost about this particular lot—a congregation split between English and Spanish speakers, middle and barely-surviving lower incomes, Pre-Vatican II believers and the newfangled modernists. So many factions dividing people who simply needed comfort. If they wanted to believe that Mary was the mother of God and appeared to some kids, that seemed okay to me. Plus, the Bosnian countryside sounded like a beautiful place. We could all use some extra beauty even if it was only in our mind's eye. He nodded his head in agreement.

Emboldened by his kindness and quick laugh, I asked him out. I wasn't sure at the moment if it was a romantic gesture or something different. It was a grown-up move regardless of motivation and I liked how it felt. Phone numbers were exchanged and we agreed to meet up the next day at a monastery in the next city over.

A monastery. Could I be any more Catholic? Geez, definitely not the setting for romance. But I followed the directions across town and then into the next one, eventually finding the lonely dirt road that led to a colorful oasis and one Peter casually leaning against the fence in a white T-shirt, faded jeans, and flip-flops, drinking a beer.

Whoa. Whoa. Whoa. What is this beer stuff? What is this place? Who is this person? Is this a cult? That's it. It's a cult. I'm going to be sacrificed in a fire. Something terrible is going to happen to me. I felt it in my bones. And yet, I parked my little Honda next to a shady tree and *almost* skipped (I had some decorum) to my new friend, who put his beer down to welcome me with a huge bear hug. If this cult meant daily bear hugs, I was ready to give up all my worldly possessions and get weird and culty.

"Hi hi hi!" He smiled at me upon release. "Welcome!"

"New friend, Peter, what is this place? Who are you?"

Peter grabbed my hand and pulled me into the compound of shady trees and flower-lined paths. The afternoon wind was picking up and instead of hucking projectiles as it did at the junkyard, here the wind seemed to gather orange blossom scent, sprinkling freshness into each step. As we ambled along colorful paths and said hello to the gaggle of Benedictine monks doing various tasks along the way, Peter explained that he, too, lived there amongst the monks. He had heard about the monastery after graduating from art school. They offered room and board to artists in exchange for help with the grounds. So Peter made his way from Austin, Texas, settled into a tiny room, and spent his day immersed in the beauty of the place and painting religious icons. At night, he and the monks cooked together, sometimes in the kitchen or out on the terrace over an elaborate barbeque, and then ate around a campfire, telling wild stories and asking questions of one another.

That first night, I fell silent listening to their laughter, a sound I hadn't heard from adults in a long time. I stopped listening to their words, and the rhythms of their hilarity filled the open space; my blood flowed calm. Funny. Sensitive. Curious. These were good people. They were not trying to prove anything or be anyone other than who they were. I would return for many more afternoons and early evenings over the next couple of months, a welcome reprieve from junkyard life as well as a stark contrast to the final months of high school, where we were all unsettled yet intent on figuring out our next chapter. Aside from my teachers at school, Peter and these monks were the only adults I knew that had been to college. Rare specimens in my world.

I remember one night around the campfire, after hitting a wall trying to write my application essays for UC Irvine and Berkeley—two schools I had wanted to go to since as long as I could remember—I allowed myself to cry in front of these men. "What's troubling you, kid?" one of them asked with a gentleness I rarely encountered. Open floodgates. Blubbering: GO! "I'm blank. I can't see. I can't feel. I'm supposed to go to college. I don't have the money for it and these applications want me to write about what I want to study and why. But I don't know." I began to sob, the emptiness of my ignorance and the darkness of my blank mental screen suffocating me from the inside out. Peter reached out for my hand, holding it in silence until the sobs subsided.

When I was ready, the men took turns telling stories of leaving their families and stumbling through adulthood and studies. Like me, most came from parents who were of a generation and social class where college was a luxurious concept rather than tangible reality. Unlike me, these men had the perspective of time and age to know that college was not the means to a job but a tool to gain knowledge.

"Robyn, try a different school. Maybe one that isn't asking you questions you can't possibly know the answers to yet," Peter softly suggested. I nodded, still not understanding what was possible, but feeling better for taking a risk and trusting these men with my fears. Over the days and weeks to follow, as I walked the paths of the monastery and went for long road trips to Joshua Tree with my new friend, fresh projections began to flow across my empty screen. It was okay to read, walk, listen to Patsy Cline, and experience the world with pleasure. This, too, was learning. It was okay to make art and write; creation was a language of its own, viable and vital. This, too, can be a job—a life's work. Not all life had to be destroyed: pulling parts, stripping metals—the currency of my family's current life. What if you made something, rather than took it away? What if you wore flip-flops and weren't worried about breaking or bloodying toes? What if you were free to love and think without being judged? What if you were free? I was learning to be free: one step, then another, barefoot, forward momentum, feeling for once, each blade of grass undertow confirming that divinity lives within and inspiration lives everywhere.

I would ask Peter to the prom, as any silly high school girl with a kinda crush would do. Totally the wrong thing to do. As the elder statesman of our two-person club, he knew this was completely inappropriate and politely declined. I had moved on from my mom's Danielle Steel romance novels to Camus and Sartre's existential perplexities, so I knew it was okay to not bet too hard on a fleeting crush, the nature of existence being somewhat unstable. What I could bet on was that although it was time to move on from this friend, his kindness and generosity would live on within me forever, helping me realize that beauty and safety were not only possible but within reach.

Chapter 15
Rights of the Bold

We were beautiful but didn't know it.

In the sea of used and abused, this was clearly a winning combination.

We loved the music, the lights erupting from darkness. The presence of those who dared. A wellspring of raw energy that made us feel alive, too. We would cram ourselves into tiny cars, find parking spots several blocks away from the club—because let's be real, we barely had enough money to get into the club (and sometimes not even that), let alone pay for parking. Then, in we went, finding a way to a dark corner, claiming the edges for our own—we hadn't earned the rights of the bold to take space in the center. Not yet, anyway. The scene: where one came to notice or be noticed. A clamoring of hope and transformation—all of us inching away from what we had been toward what would forever shape us. Hollywood was like that.

So, when Grandma pulled out the typewriter and the pad of onion typing papers, plopping them down on the dining room table with a puff of cigarette smoke, I wasn't exactly warm to her unglamorous direction. I wanted to go out and see! Be seen! But Grandma said, "If you are going to live here, you need a real job. Learn."

I had recently moved in with my grandmother—my mom's mother—after languishing in bed for days, unable to move from under the heaviness of being seventeen, graduated, and wanting to move forward but not knowing how to go about it. One morning, I had awakened before dawn, gasping for air and yearning to shed the weight— the realization that it was time to move on (a sign that has guided me in the years since). My family's outpost in the high desert felt so far away from all that I treasured: music, art, and ocean… and work, so that I could pay for my first year of college in the fall. I had recently learned that my college fund was gone, another unknown weighing me down. I wasn't mad. My family needed the money to get by, but it meant that I needed to get hustling.

My grandmother, on the other hand, was ideally situated in the heart of Orange County in Anaheim, minutes away from the beach, record stores, and the allure of Hollywood. At that point, location was all I needed to kickstart my life. Grandma was less enthusiastic, frowning a no before smirking a yes. We didn't really know one another and she was lonely, so why not.

We were a doomed partnership from the beginning. I arrived with my blue Honda Civic filled to the brim with my record collection, posters to decorate my new "adult" space, and piles of clothes. She put on her best face—a deeply powdered and coral-lipped facade—welcoming me into her "home," a mobile home situated next to the 5 Freeway that looked cheery enough on the outside thanks to the yellow and white facade and a lemon tree that shared its blossoms and fruit in her tiny yard. Seemed cute enough. But as soon she opened the sliding door, I knew I was trespassing on a life she had been intent on keeping to herself. She looked over my head as if scanning for threats before she silently waved me in.

Hesitant, I followed her into the dark trailer. There was no light in there. Each room was weighed down by bulky furniture and the scent of stale cigarettes. Dark green carpet shagged across the floors. I would soon learn never to walk barefoot, as it was often damp with Teddy the poodle's pee, impossible to find in the darkness until you stepped right in it. The only color could be found on the walls in a series of oil-painted clowns sneering at me as I made my way to my new room.

"Settle in and then we'll make dinner," she instructed. More clowns sneered at me from above the bed. Yeah, settle in, little lady, they mocked. The room was not vacant and they knew it. Lining the walls, hiding under the bed, and filling the bureau were the belongings of my grandmother's second husband. He might have been securely confined in a federal penitentiary in Arizona, but the remains of his life were archived in that room. Stacks of horse racing tips, ledger sheets running black and then red, and most disturbingly, hundreds of sex books... the joy of it and otherwise. I shut the door behind me and found my grandmother for dinner. A gourmet feast of greasy hamburger meat in a corn tortilla and a side of canned three-bean salad awaited me.

I had come too far to run back home. It could be an epic summer, the first away from my family and the junkyard. I needed to make it work at all costs. So, I settled in and we found our groove: ironing on Sundays for her work week at the phone company; strange concoctions for dinner (she was not a cook and I was equally as helpless); martinis for her real dinner (heavy on the vodka, a hint of vermouth); typing practice for me; and then bed. In the mornings, I would wait to emerge from my room, listening for her morning rituals: manicured fingernails tapping on the kitchen counter; a cigarette sparked to life, followed by a long inhale and exhale; footsteps back to the bedroom to don her pre-selected blouse and skirt from Sunday's ironing marathon; a trip into the bathroom to apply the face—coral lipstick, mascara, penciled eyebrows—and then the hair, short silver strands hair sprayed into place. She would stomp her five-foot-ten frame down the hallway, intent on making sure that she woke me and that I was not being a lazy, ungrateful teenager.

Then finally, the best sound of the day: the slam of the door. As her teal Cadillac pulled out of the carport, I would jump out of bed with relief, quickly pet Teddy, get dressed, drag piles of her husband's stuff that was cluttering "my" room to the dumpster, and then hit the road, eager to find a job that did not involve typing. My strategy was simple: I would drive up and down streets I deemed cool, looking for record stores or boutiques that might need a helping hand like mine. The search was slow going, but I didn't care because it meant I had more radio time—the other great advantage of this central locale, alternative radio stations from L.A. *and* San Diego. Truth was, I didn't care if I ever found a job. If only I could spend my days like that: listening to the newest music, meeting cute musician boys, and calling the day good by watching the setting sun at Huntington Beach. My summer was shaping up nicely.

~ X ~

A few weeks went on with our new routine. I didn't know what to make of that woman, nor did I know how to talk to her. The feeling was mutual, as I discovered in letters to and from her imprisoned husband. I was always looking for clues to who she was, so I was quick on the draw to get to the mail first. Squinting my eyes, I could make out paragraphs through the envelopes. If a sentence struck me as too ridiculous, I took that as a sign to steam it open and see what swill was about to intoxicate Grandma with irritation toward me. These stolen weekly letters provided some insight. "Teenagers are rotten and can't be trusted. Don't take any shit. She's probably a whore, most teenage girls are," he wrote.

Funny—from a man in prison for racketeering, among other charges. Funny—from a man who had leaned over the front seat of the Cadillac that dark night so long ago, still adjusting the zipper on his pants, negotiating the silence of seven-year-old me. Funny—from a man who, later that night, snuck out to my guest spot on the couch, crushing my small body with his, the framed clown paintings looking down at us from every surrounding wall, their wide-eyed painted faces glowing and sinister and goofy.

Funny how it all came back, just like that day I'd first visited the junkyard all those years ago. But in this room, it wasn't a memory of how I learned to be strong. It was pure memory of the scene: the violence. The smell. The sweat of him. And now, night after night, I was in a room with all his things. Even though I took a few piles of the sex books and gambling ledgers to the dumpster every day, I couldn't erase him, or a growing paranoia about my grandma. Did she know what he did to me all those years ago? Did he hurt others? Did he hurt her? I wanted to ask her, but didn't know how.

One night, after many sleepless nights, I couldn't take the obsessive thoughts any longer and I took a swing: "Grandma, did you know… did you know that something bad happened to me when I was a kid?" My voice got small. I wasn't sure if she even heard me.

A moment or two passed. She lit a cigarette, and then on the exhale: "Did your dad do something? He was always so mean to you kids." My dad? Compared to her husband, my dad was an angel.

"No, someone else…" I faltered. "It's just that sometimes I think about it at night and I can't sleep. And then I get really sad." I couldn't say his name, nor did I mention that *sometimes* meant most nights, and that I had been dipping into her vodka to dull the sharpness of the memories. She was not interested in this conversation, and wandered off without another word to iron a blouse for her work day. I would never bring it up again, hoping that she did not know, hoping that she would have saved me if she did, hoping that she didn't go silent to save face. I wanted to be brave and tell her, but in those dark, vodka-infused nights, I was more afraid that she would not care.

～ X ～

On some nights, when one martini turned to four, Grandma would sink into her recliner listening to Frank Sinatra. Those were the good nights. Sloppy, yes. But she'd follow story threads back to a time before marrying a con artist with ties to organized crime; before the devastating death of her first husband, a decorated marine, who had been much beloved in his community and worshiped by his family. The movie reel in her mind spun in reverse, back to a time before giving birth to her four children (my mom, her firstborn), before wars, to a time when she, too, used to dance in Hollywood clubs, under the lights, coiffed and elegant. There was a glow beyond the booze as she actually looked me in the eye and held my gaze, making sure her stories landed. Her early years of glamour and good old-fashioned fun—this was when she knew exactly who she was: not beholden to anyone or anything; beautiful and just beginning.

I eventually found that non-typing job: much to Grandma's disapproval, I worked full time—as a clerk in a record store. It was a cool job, and allowed me to save up enough for my first year of college and many, many nights out. That summer was filled with ups and downs as my grandmother and I danced around one another's expectations—too experienced and not experienced enough to have any degree of meaningful connection. She would often lock me out if I came home too late or if she caught a sniff of the Teddy-masking incense I'd burned earlier, sure it was weed.

I'd knock at the carport door hoping she'd take pity on me. "Grandma, it's me. I'm so sorry." But she would never let me in. I suspect she was standing on the other side of the door, shaking her head with annoyance. Tough love in action. With a mix of shame and defiance, I would march my way to the small parking lot twenty yards from her sliding door to sleep in the backseat of my car, a backdrop of never-ending traffic on I5 to keep me company. If I was feeling feisty, I'd turn on the music and drive to my parents' house seventy miles away to sleep in my old bed. That was a risk, though, because then I would have to explain to my mom that I was out late again and driving her mother insane, and that a phone call of complaint from Grandma was imminent.

Later, a couple of years after I graduated from college, Grandma's husband was released from prison at age seventy-one. His newfound freedom was short-lived. With a pellet gun tucked in his Members Only jacket, he held up a local Wells Fargo bank and then proceeded to lead the police on a slow-speed chase in grandma's old teal

Cadillac back to her trailer. He parked, slowly got out of the car, and pointed the gun at the police. The police, in turn, shot to kill. My roommates and I watched it on the news in silence.

> "We didn't even know it was [a pellet gun] until the crime lab people came and picked it up and examined it," Lt. LaBahn said. "As an officer in the field, if it looks like a handgun, smells like a handgun, you can't wait to look down the barrel to see if it's real. It's too late by then."
>
> –From the article "Slain Suspect Had Prior Robbery Conviction," *Los Angeles Times*, August 21, 1996

It was through the news and newspaper articles that I learned of the trouble this man had caused my grandmother over the years. Robberies, bad checks, taking out dozens of credit cards in her name only to max them out. Run-ins with the mafia. Grandma had continued to work well past retirement because of the financial turmoil he had created for her. But the documented crime had nothing on the fear she lived with, never knowing if a loan shark's threat would come to pass. At one point, her beloved poodle Josephine's eye was removed by some gangsters as a message of what might befall her should they not pay up for gambling debts. The death of her husband was less loss and more relief. She wasn't of a generation to complain, or at least, complain too much.

Her role was to survive, and that often meant donning full armor to keep everyone out—or simply adapting to a new set of circumstances.

I began to understand.

My hurts had nothing on hers.

Instead of asking her more questions I knew she didn't want to answer, I started over, writing her monthly letters about my *adult-ish* life. She in turn, shared stories from her life when she was in her late teens and early twenties, matching my themes of toiling through work days as a means to get to fun—whatever and wherever it could be had.

> *May 10th, 2000*
>
> *Dear Robyn,*
> *Guess it's about time that I quit procrastinating & put my thoughts on paper again. The postcards that you sent of the cherry blossoms are so beautiful. You've really seen some beautiful scenery, haven't you?*
>
> *Glad to hear that you'll be coming back in August… I know that your mom and dad are anxious & wish you were coming there instead of Portland.*
>
> *I have some pretty good, very old memories of Portland. I lived there for about a year and a half after I graduated from high school. Had a lot of fun there. My first semester of college was in Seattle. I missed the second ¼ and played a lot…*

My mom's Aunt Kate, a "spinster" from Ireland, owned a house there [in Portland on SE 17th near St. Philip Neri Church]. She lived on the first floor & we lived on the second. She was a tyrant & not too easy to get along with. What a character! She eloped with Tim Dorgan, also from Ireland, when they were 70 years old!!!!

I had quite a few friends in Gresham & spent a lot of time there. The boys had Model A Fords & a couple of motorcycles. The girls had no cars. Rode on a few of the motorcycles & went to a lot of hill climbs. Did a lot of riding around in those Model As—like to Salem for ice cream & Astoria for fresh crab. Loved the coast line. That's where I learned to drive! In one of those Model As.

After that I stomped the streets looking for a job. No such luck. So I came back to Calif. & was at work within 3 weeks. Good old telephone company. So much for my fun days in Portland...

Believe it! I will be 80! Don't feel that old, however. In fact, I feel great & very lucky! Health is good. Like your advice "smile at least 10 times a day"—I smile all the time...

That's it for this time. More later.

All my love,
Grandma

How do you move forward when your world has ended? You decide that your world is simply beginning again.

I began to understand.

Our hurts can heal.

For a brief interlude, we were equals in our reveries: faces painted, lips red, aglow under the lights, emboldened by more than the music. We were strong and we knew it.

Grandma and my Aunt Kathy, 2/26/2000

Chapter 16
Hungry

"Hey! Do you want a sandwich?" My dad was waving his arms, yelling at me from below in his high-pitched squeal, the special Harry voice reserved for being excited or talking to children or animals. Do I want a sandwich? I looked down at my belly. *Now, that's a crazy question isn't it?* When are impoverished college students not hungry?

"Pastrami on a kaiser roll with alfalfa sprouts and pickles, please. So hungry. Thanks Dad!" I shouted down from the top of a dilapidated RV, impact drill in hand, so caked in dirt I no longer remembered what I was wearing when I left my rented room earlier that morning. It was a Holy Saturday, but the customers forgot to show up again. So, to make my 35-mile drive worthwhile from San Bernardino, I was doing stuff and things.

Stuff and things like standing on top of an ancient RV, removing rivets, yanking off molding and wiring, and separating various metals into containers to be recycled at the scrap yard down the street. Worthless bits over here. Money bits over there. Steel versus aluminum. Copper wire—boom, what a score. In this moment I was critically aware that I was no better than the tweakers roaming the aisles stealing whatever they could, but I turned the thought off in my brain as quickly as I could to avoid the shame. This effort might just get me over the finish line to pay rent and have enough to spare for a night out. There was a band I wanted to see that night at a tiny club in Riverside called Spanky's, and if I busted through this pile sooner rather than later, I would have enough time to de-grease and glamorize to make it happen. And now that I had a sandwich, maybe two, coming my way, I felt invincible.

Today's endeavor was mindless work that vacillated between being calming and soul-crushing, not to mention nerve-damaging. The impact drill was becoming a big part of my Saturdays with Dad. This tool of the trade was the go-to to tear anything apart when efficiency was valued over precision. And we were never about precision. My cold fingers would hold on for dear life as I jabbed the drill into radiator cores, motors, odd metal contraptions, and RVs—the handle vibrating, shaking all feeling from my hands. By the end of the day, I would struggle to bend my fingers or even grab the steering wheel so I could drive home. Every time, I would swear that I would not come back—that I needed to finally be a college student doing college student things, like studying and amping up the hours at all my other jobs. But sure enough, every Saturday morning I would return with a fresh need to fill my coffers and hopefully, be of help to my dad.

My dad, who by 6 a.m. was already hustling for the day, tearing into heaps of metal with his own impact drill, knowing that the customers were probably not going to come if the preceding weeks and months were any indicator. But maybe, maybe they would. Maybe someone would randomly stop by to buy a motor or a transmission. A big ticket item that would bring some ease to the day. He could stop rummaging through all the metal piles and shouting for an hour or two. It would mean his pocket would be full of cash and my mom would smile at him when he returned home in the evening. They could celebrate by going out to dinner and eat whatever they wanted without complaint, unless the service was bad, and then there would be complaining.

But I would be long gone before then and didn't need to consider the rude words and grunting that could potentially be unleashed on the unsuspecting waiter, who would beg another waiter to take over for him, and if begging didn't work, tip money would be exchanged to dodge this particular Harry bullet. No, I needed to focus on the present. If Harry could do this day after day, surely I could sacrifice a few hours of my pride, too. Better yet, I would Jedi mind trick myself:

Harry is your inspiration.
Harry has been putting food on the table for over forty years.
Harry knows how to survive.
What have you done, hungry Robyn?
Be tough like Harry.
Don't yell at people, though. That's uncool.

Can you be cool, Robyn?
I believe in you.
Turn off your brain and be cool.
Be cool.
Be cool.
No, don't look at the tweakers.
DON'T LOOK. Not over there!
Back to your RV.
Your sandwich is coming soon.
Don't think about your hands.
I know you can't feel your fingers anymore.
It will be over soon.
Be cool.
Sandwich.
Survive like Harry.

～ ✕ ～

Survival has many looks. My biggest step for survival in those days was to find a college that would accept me without making me decide a major. I shelved my UC applications and applied to a state school that would allow me to stumble all over the map. Cal State San Bernardino was the only school I applied to, and luckily, they let me in. I loved my studies. And they were indeed all over the map: art, art history, literature, anthropology, geology, and French by way of translated literature. I loved the campus with its shady trees and the San Bernardino National Forest lurking in its backdrop. I loved my new best friend and sister in arms, Elle, who I met in the world's most boring geology class. I loved working at the campus radio station, the multicultural center, the cafe down the street, and even for a short time, a fancy auto recycling business where I was responsible for all the odd jobs, like going to the bank, picking up lunch, and getting kitty litter for oil spills and trying not to get mugged while doing it (I was not always successful at this).

I even loved my little rented room with its sweet childish pink-flowered wallpaper and the bookshelf that extended all the way around overhead, knocking tomes onto my head whenever the San Andreas fault became angry and shook us with all her might. Later, I would score my own apartment that was within cycling distance to campus, falling in love with its grown-up attached garage and patio for flowers. What I loved less was that I was hungry. Even though I added job after job to my week, there was never enough money to go around for all the expenses and to feed my insatiable appetite for, well, everything. I was in a constant state of moving forward and taking ten steps back inevitably to my family and the junkyard, where nothing and yet everything was the same.

I wanted my family to be impressed by who I was becoming, mainly so I would feel less guilty about the good times I was having while they toiled away. I was fancy. I danced on Tuesday nights and saw bands on Friday and Saturday nights. I watched films in *French*. I was obsessed with Tolstoy. I wrote poetry and performed funny pieces at spoken word nights. People laughed with rather than at me. I was funny; there was clapping!

I liked brie. I had a boyfriend who had a different skin color than mine. Sadly, I had credit cards and could be a grown up in that way, too, buying whatever I wanted to much consequence. On some days, I think my family was slightly impressed. But on most days, it was as if we were speaking different languages. Plus, undergraduate students—especially liberal arts ones—are insufferable. I was no exception to the rule. Brie, Tolstoy, Black boyfriend, ridiculous vintage clothing habit, and existential considerations had no place in the junkyard. Who did I think I was? Where was their daughter and sister?

Where was I? In no-woman's land, the kingdom reserved for the time period when you don't know what you don't know. It was the early nineties. Still pre-internet and without the ability to Google all the important things like:

- *What do you do with a liberal arts degree?*
- *Mo' money jobs?*
- *How long can you put off paying back student loans?*
- *Best cheap eats? Like under $5, please.*
- *Shows in L.A. Go!*
- *Shows in San Diego. Go!*
- *Shows in Inland Empire. Go!*
- *Is Betsey Johnson on Melrose having a sale?*
- *What do you do when your boyfriend is a drug addict and you didn't know because you were busy going to college and working 100 jobs?*

- *What do you do when your brother is a drug addict and you kinda knew but you were busy going to college and working 100 jobs?*
- *Best way to move out of an apartment when your boyfriend, who you don't really like anymore and maybe never did but needed a roommate, is at work.*
- *What do you do if your boyfriend pulls a gun on you?*
- *Is it wrong if you don't care if your boyfriend dies or not?*
- *How do you get a restraining order?*
- *How do you thank your dad for helping you move out of your own apartment during the daytime without him thinking you're an idiot?*
- *Can you die from shame?*
- *Can you be different from your family and still be loved and love back?*
- *Can you drink too much?*
- *What is too much?*
- *What are the pretty blooming trees in my neighborhood?*
- *How do you travel in Europe on $5?*

My only tool for information was the library and these subjects were not represented well in the catalog system. So, classic Robyn, I kept my problems to myself and continued to stumble forward, soaking up the good things and attempting to shove all the unsavory things to a dark corner of my mind. I found myself splitting my life again: my default coping mechanism that I relied on so heavily during adolescence. My college life was different from my job life which was different from my going-out life or the one back home with my family. I was juggling and attempting to collect what felt right to me, dropping balls all over the place. The contrast to my oldest life—my family—was a growing divide. Maybe it was because I was exhausted, or maybe because this particular skin shed was so different, that I felt more adrift and judged. Looking back, it all makes sense, given the amount of new experiences and influences, but at the time it was jarring and came with a crushing loneliness.

Toward the end of my college tenure, I became one compartment lighter. I was about to be dethroned as junkyard princess—or maybe better put, I took off my crown, put it in a box, and never considered it an option again. A choice. One that, looking back, was so obvious to make and yet I held on for longer than I should have. For what, I still don't know. At one point in my early twenties, saddled on my high horse, I decided I would take over the junkyard. I'd learned things in my newly-minted adult life. I could help. I drafted business plans and financial projections. My offer was initially met with relief, but it became clear that my half-hearted efforts were an insult to my dad's dreams and his place within them. I was no longer an insider with the secret handshake. I heard them—my dad, brother, yard guys, and resident tweakers—talk about me and my stupid charts, graphs, and projections:

"What did the college girl know about anything? Stupid bitch." I overheard some iteration of my ignorance over and over again. There was no kindness left, their words cruel and brittle.

One afternoon, I made the drive up from school. I had a rare day off from my main job and oddly, I wanted to see my dad. Sometimes when I was feeling down, a visit with my dad and the promise of a sandwich made me feel better. It was always a crapshoot because I could catch him in the middle of one of his reigns of terror, in which case he might call me names and I would leave feeling more dejected. But if I was lucky, I would catch him when he needed me the most, too, and he would be glad for my company, especially over a sandwich.

I was optimistic (and hungry) as I pulled into the parking lot and made my way through the towering gate and then the front door of the office. The office was empty. My mom's old desk was covered with parts and scraps of paper holding notes from old phone calls. The yellow counter, too, was piled high with parts and far dirtier than I'd have kept it. The microwave door was left open, the inside cavern a slough of discarded food and unidentifiable sludge. The floors were covered in grime. I steered clear of the bathroom. None of the phone receivers were in their respective cradles, but were left dangling from their cords. All signs that something was not right. I should have stopped and made a beeline for the parking lot. I could see my dad another day. Another day in which

I could summon the ambition to get the office back in order and be helpful.

But instead I slipped past the yellow counter, looking for my dad like I had since I was a little girl. Just as I opened the door to the warehouse, a tall man covered in grit and grease grabbed the door handle from the other side and shoved the door in my face. Whoa. Who was this guy? He must have made a mistake. Doesn't he know who I *am*? I grabbed the handle again for attempt number two only to be greeted by a snarl. "Bitch, get the fuck out."

I squinted my eyes. Do I know this person? Does he know me? Is this a random *Bitch, get the fuck out* or a targeted one?

I did not know that person, or at least, if I did at some point, he was no longer recognizable to me. Rotting teeth. Sunken eyes. Dirty skin covered in sores. A cold calm washed over me. My inner junkyard princess would not be told what to do. I shoved the door back, "Where the fuck is my dad, asshole?" The cold calm was on the move. I felt the change in my words and stance, fury building, making me tall. I couldn't stop now.

"This is my business. Where is my dad?" I repeated.

He yanked the door out of my hand and stepped toward me, his wiry body radiating stank. I didn't move. He stepped within an inch of my face, lips moving, sound sputtering out: "GET. THE. FUCK. OUT. OF. HERE. BITCH." He raised his hand as if to hit me and only then did I back down, running to my car as fast as I could. I turned my brain off. Must. Get. Out. Something. Is. Wrong. Very.

Wrong. I jumped into my car, stabbed the key in the ignition with shaky hands, and then peeled out into the street, flooring it as soon as I stabilized.

As I turned the corner, I looked back at the junkyard. The guy had jumped into a beater car and was following me. I slammed my foot on the gas only to find him matching my speed. He was only a few feet behind me. I went faster, sliding around on the dirt road trying to get to a more populated area as quickly as possible. Finally, I made it to Main Street, making a right into civilization, my heart pounding. *I am safe.* I checked the rearview mirror. He paused and then flipped a U-turn. And just like that, he was gone. I did not call the police. Instead, I continued with my right turn, taking Main Street to the freeway, down the Cajon Pass, and back to my new life.

I never learned who this person was or what they were up to. Nameless, Faceless Grease Monster is what I call him in my memories. I obviously interrupted something I shouldn't have. When I am most gracious, I like to think that he was scaring me to safety so that I wouldn't get caught in the middle of whatever danger was unfolding for the day.

I am still embarrassed by the incident, although I don't know why. Maybe for what it might say about my family and where I am now from. We were not criminals or bad people and yet these people were everywhere on our property, in our city, and scattered throughout the desert. We were doing the best we could under the circumstances. My parents were doing the best they could. Good people caught up in tough times. Mantras repeated like fingers stroking beads on a rosary string. I never asked my dad or my brother any questions about that day. There are some answers that are not helpful. There are some answers that I do not want to know—answers that would declare all our work and the better times, null and void.

I would never see the monster again.

The junkyard would limp along a few more years but I would never set foot there again.

My reign as junkyard princess had come to an end.

⌣ ✕ ⌢

Not too long ago, I was eyeballing one of the bookshelves in my dining room and my eyes landed on a very old edition of *The Complete Poems and Plays of T.S. Eliot*. "Where did you come from, old friend?" I asked, blowing off its dusty layer and then fanning it open only to find a parking ticket from my undergrad days. Actually, an "almost" parking ticket, as it had this note:

> ROBYN SAUNDERS,
> WHY DON'T YOU HAVE A DECAL? J/K YOU SEXY, EXOTIC ARTISTIC WOMAN YOU! GOOD THING I SAW YOUR NAME ON YOUR BILL BACK SEAT—GTE. HAVE A NICE DAY!! --ERIC L.

Evidently, I had a friend on parking patrol who noticed what was probably an unpaid utility bill hanging out on my back seat and wrote me a love note instead of a violation. Thank god—these were some lean years. I barely had enough change for a cup of coffee let alone another parking ticket.

Yes, *another*. If it wasn't a parking ticket, it was a speeding ticket. If it wasn't a speeding ticket, it was a broken taillight or some other safety infraction. I seemed to specialize in offense and recklessness and hunger. I wanted to go forward and fast, but the rules, man… always getting in the way of my velocity.

Anyways, back to T.S. Eliot. A couple of days after finding the dusty copy, I came across a slimmer version of the *Four Quartets*, hiding in my basement office. A message from the poetry gods? Maybe ol' T.S. himself? I'm a sucker for these poems—four reflections on memory, time, and the human quest to find meaning. During my senior year in college, I took a seminar on Eliot, a rare treat to spend an entire quarter exclusively on one writer. On the first day of the course, our professor asked us how we had come across Eliot, as this work wasn't exactly easy reading or accessible. My classmates, per the usual of any lit class, pontificated and puffed forth because everyone in their twenties knows absolutely everything about everything. In my own pretentious way, I did the same, offering that my mom had Eliot's poetry laying around. You know, as one does. A little T.S. Eliot next to the fire alongside the complete works of Whitman, Whittier, and Dickinson to round out the mix.

My professor was impressed. It was a stretch, but it wasn't completely untrue. What I left off in all my puffery was that I had learned of Eliot through a historical romance novel. My mom was an avid reader, and her collection of books offered a portal to history, art, and great writers—albeit through Danielle Steel and Susan Howatch—but still, I got there. And it was through Howatch that I found Eliot, his thoughts and verse woven through juicy family dramas spanning decades and hundreds of sexy pages. No doubt my classmates would have found this decidedly lowbrow entry point an affront to their complex sensibilities; however, like many kids of my generation, I suspect that's how most of them came across the "greats," too. Honesty wasn't exactly a seminar tactic. Honesty is only something that comes with time, when you no longer have to resort to puffery for status. Honesty and its buddy, curiosity, plus time—these are our tools for connecting the dots and making sense of the world at large and our place in it.

And so, amidst a pile of new parking tickets (old habits die hard), volumes of poetry, and juicy novels, I get the benefit of middle age to find the patterns, to learn and unlearn who I am. I get the benefit of my mom's reading, which inspired my own love—T.S. Eliot would eventually take me to Claremont, California, where I would seek out stories of his lover, Emily Hale, a Scripps College professor of the past. And in Claremont, I would meet love redefined: my mentor, Kirk Delman, who kindly allowed me to work in the art collection at Scripps College and helped me settle into just being me. We would move art together, prepare galleries for shows, talk about trees and birds, wonder at the beauty, rail against those who refused to see it. He would show me how to slow down, drink coffee at all hours of the day, and never say no to a biscotti. He would encourage me to travel. In other words, he would show me how to live.

And, I would meet a certain graduate student who I would secretly marry one day on my lunch break—who, just a few months later, would move with me to Japan and then finally to Oregon to begin anew.

It was on my husband's front stoop in 1998 that I would begin telling my junkyard story. Side by side with the bright sun on our faces, his hand covering mine, I tried to say all the words I had never been able to say. Without a church to confess my transgressions of not doing enough or a family home to wrap myself in sanctuary, the story I blurted out started with the end: my parents giving back the keys to the former owners earlier that day, unable to move forward. The anticlimactic end was finally at hand, waiting for their reinvention while I proceeded with mine.

Chapter 17
Let Me Tell You a Story

"Let me tell you a story."

My dad begins again inches away from my face, his glasses so thick that I think he's lost the plot on all spatial perception. This is going to be a good one, he tells me, excitedly rubbing his thick hands together as if he needs a warm up. I can tell by the wide shape of his eyes and the almost-upturn of the left side of his thin lips that he thinks whatever comes next is going to be funny. I can tell by the way my face settles into its neutral position and I begin regulating my breath, slowing my heart rate, that I've heard this one before. At fifty, my muscle memory is fortified in strength and knows exactly what to do.

"Tell me a story, Dad." I extend a small smile. No teeth. No laughter. I have to pace myself for a weekend of moments like this, conserving as much energy as possible for his non-sequitur outbursts that demand the room and are not interested in a back and forth. He talks over all voices in his one-sided way. Today's story is no different. He launches into an often-told tale from the early 1960s, of helping his own father on a strange job in Susanville, California—an old mining, logging, and freight transportation hub, now known for being a federal prison site, all industry long gone. I mentally check out, having heard this particular story so many times, so I am thrown off when his voice changes to a cruel bark and I hear, "Robyn, did you kick him out? Yes or no?"

I can tell he's referring to Justin, my brother's son and now my bonus child for the past seven years. At twenty-one, Justin is no longer a boy and not quite an adult: a defiant in-between with his own apartment, a stash of Top Ramen, a job, and dreams of grandeur. My body tells me my dad's anger is about to escalate. My muscle memory is finely tuned—my exhales automatically get longer to keep calm, telling my heart to hold up, we're going to get into it, but we're safe. We are nimble. We can drive away if we need to.

"What do you think, Dad? It sounds like you know the answer to your question." I hear the coldness in my tone, but a heat rising within. He does not blink, his eyes dark marbles. I see the familiar door close, me on one side, my dad on the other. He has made an assumption and I am not to be trusted. I am one of *those* women, just like his mom who so long ago left him behind—the heartless type who leaves. He does not know the first thing about the answer to his question—the reality of what he is asking—but has decided to jump to certain conclusions anyway.

༄ ✕ ༄

"Robyn, can I tell you a story?" A tiny, garbled voice from the seat next to me breaks my focus. Justin is thirteen, although he looks closer to seven or eight checking in at about seventy-five pounds. His bright blue eyes are sad even when he laughs or tells a funny story. I keep doing a double-take, his white blonde hair confusing me, bringing up memories of my brother at this age. Other than his sadness, I don't see traces of his mother; a small kindness to the boy—she has been dead for three months and without the likeness, he does not have to see her memory every time he looks in the mirror. He and my mom are visiting my family in Oregon for the week and I just took him mountain biking for the first time. We are covered in mud, an immediate messy dusting of kinship.

"Heck yeah, tell me a story." I smile at him and we both laugh as dirt falls off my bottom lip. We did a great job tearing up the trail.

Over the years, Justin will tell many stories. Some true. Some wild and decidedly untrue. Some he will believe. Others he will simply relish in living out the imaginary details. But it is this first story, one that is not mine to tell, that will change both of our lives forever. I will listen as he shares through sobs, shaking in his seat. I know not to pull over, to touch him, to reach out and scoop him in my arms. I know that comfort for this type of hurt needs safety first. I know to wait until the emotion subsides, and simply ask, "Do you want to live with us?"

The answer is in the relief I see flash across his face.

Calls are made. Tense conversations completed. Guardianship papers drawn up. My mom is sent back to California without him, changing our relationship forever. I know it is the right thing to do, the difference between life and death, to keep this boy, even if it means upending every single one of my relationships and in some cases, severing ties forever.

― ✕ ―

There are small signs at first, but we write them off as a boy who has just endured unimaginable pain and trauma and has lived in chaos for the past thirteen years. He doesn't know how to control himself yet. "It's okay," we say, "there's just more learning to do." So, we stumble forward, finding ways to help him navigate big emotions. We laugh, ride bikes, walk for miles, and run off the big things. We slow down, learn not to react to the small things. School happens. For him, letters are recognizable but then disappear. Numbers are backward. Instructions make little to no sense.

He remains good-humored for the most part, but his frustration is evident as his understanding wobbles between extremes. We do testing so that we can understand how to support him; so he can understand what is happening on the inside even when his body is miraculous—riding and running at top speeds, winning races, collecting medals that his doctors say shouldn't be possible. He will graduate from high school, even gain a scholarship to college. We are defying all odds. We are winning until we aren't.

༺ ✕ ༻

"You left me."

A guard stands outside his door, listening for an uptick in mood.

I sit back in the metal chair. This cold, inhumane chair in the corner. With the exception of running out to get a very bad chicken sandwich from Burger King, I have been in this chair around the clock, holding vigil, waiting for whatever is supposed to be next. I keep him safe, translating the doctor's complex questions; fighting when he cannot. He looks tiny in his hospital gown, with his electric blue eyes staring. Unblinking.

"I want to go home."

"I want to go home."

"I want to go home."

The first sounds strong.

The second, a childish wail, followed by hysteria.

"I just wanted help," he cries.

I know. I wanted that, too.

I see now that "help" is not an agreed-upon principle. He is eighteen years old and the past has officially caught up to him. He is no longer the tiny thirteen-year-old boy who came to live with us after his mother died. Five years of stability had provided a cushion between him and the sadness: a childhood of disappointment, interspersed neglect, fetal alcohol syndrome, and of course, the death of his mother. The onset of adulthood and the threat of the COVID-19 pandemic was enough to shake it all loose and taunt the voices that had lay dormant. And now, the voices visit him. Shadows lurk in every room, watching. They push and prod him, guiding him toward windows and bridges.

Jump, they say. *You do not belong here.* His hands curl into fists, and sometimes around knives. *Be done with it*, they say, taunting him from the corners, shady figures and voices only he can hear. He is stuck between fighting back and turning the violence toward himself.

"J, I always come back. Always. We've got to figure this out." And so begins our real journey through systems well-intentioned, but fatally flawed. "Stay. You belong here," I whisper, trying to hide that I have no idea if there are any alternatives.

Part of raising a Justin means drawing heavily on the lessons learned from being raised by a Harry Saunders. We meet him where he's at rather than creating unfair comparisons to others in his peer group, even when he can't do that himself. Having challenges doesn't mean he can't excel on fronts that belong solely to him. Justin is a constant reminder of my dad in speech pattern, ability to tell terrible nonsensical stories, fumbling when words and situations can't be processed, and an explosive temper topped off with a need to save face. On some karmic plane, raising a Justin feels like traveling back in time and pressing re-replay on the "raising a Harry" button.

"She loved you so much," I tell Justin of his mother again and again over the years. Words I wish I knew to tell my father to ease his suffering. To my dad, they probably wouldn't have rung true, but now that I see this pattern, how the scars of a mother welt but don't wither, I wish I could have done more to slow down this particular pattern from forming, before bruising one generation and then another and then another. I close my eyes, remembering a darkened house, off a dusty road perched on a hill in the middle of the desert.

It is 2005. Windows broken, mattresses on the floor, limp bodies stirring under covers. A little boy with big blue eyes clutches his mother. She is everything to him. I survey the dirty diapers and rotting food taking over all the surfaces. This is not enough neglect for anyone to intervene just yet. There are rules. Those in charge of children have said so. Those blue eyes. Searching, seeing everything but unable to process. When she dies a decade later, those blue eyes are left to wonder about all the whys, a mind fragmented between story and reality. In the end, they are both the same, so I reassure him he was loved. She would want him to know this.

She would also want him to live even if she could not do the same for herself, her mind and body swaddled in disease and on its own timetable.

And so I help Justin course-correct, steering away from the path of his mother and father, fighting biology and history every step of the way. That's the soundbyte—the do-gooder hero's journey. But the truth is something messier. There is no end in sight. No light at the end of the tunnel. There is no "aha" moment that will make everything okay. There are finally doctors available after cold calling hundreds to no avail; there are meds always on the move, helping the gaps in his mind shrink temporarily so that he can go through the motions of "normal" life; so that his emotions are less freighted, buying moments of ease. We are tethered, he and I, in a partnership of survival. It is never enough.

I am told by his doctors that I should not think this, that he would not be alive had we not stepped in. But what of the quality of this life? I clutch at moments of safety and beauty, long walks and bike rides, absorbing the details of the natural world—wild purpled camas of spring, the return of hummingbirds, trees once bare now dripping with leaves that will drop in a few short months. The cycles of life and death and all in between inviting me to simply accept what is. In the face of the worst of it—the yelling, the violent mood swings, and delusions—I do just that. I accept and remain calm. My face and voice are neutral until it passes and he has moved on to the next thing.

I will avoid my husband's eyes, so sorry for the intrusion into the beautiful life we made together. I will explain to my daughter later. I will tell her that I am not being abused. I am not weak. Instead, this is what I must do to keep us safe. It is a mixed message of *Never let anyone under any circumstance abuse you* coupled with *We must have compassion for those who struggle with reality.* A blurred line that I am not modeling well. At night, once all are asleep, I slip outside under the moon and stars, imagining them looking down on my tiny body. One speck of a larger picture. Not insignificant, but not exactly significant either.

The day-to-day is exhausting for all involved. Some days are pure torture and yet, watching him learn to be independent and not completely beholden to his past is a worthy labor of what I like to say is love, but I think might be something else. Something more primitive, out of reach of good and bad; of love and hate. A connective tissue constantly evolving.

So Dad, to answer your question, No, I did not kick this kid out into the street.

I did not and will not abandon him.

His future is not your past.

I am your daughter; not your mother or her mother before.

I showed him what you showed me.

It is possible to work hard and proudly make choices on how you want to live.

It is possible to kick challenges in the head.

It is possible to begin to understand a brain impacted by the past.

It is possible to find peace.

It is possible even when the path forward is not well defined.

It is possible, but only if you keep asking questions.

Success will be measured by his yardstick alone.

✧

Let me tell you a story.

Once upon a time, there was a family with the last name of Story. But trouble came with that name, so they changed it to Saunders and moved far away. The trouble chilled out for a bit, but not for long, because trouble doesn't like to be hidden. She likes to smirk and kick and yell. Who can blame her? No one likes to be dismissed.

When I married, I kept trouble's disguise of Saunders, becoming a hyphenator, to honor this idea that we can move forward and become anyone we want. A misguided strategy if there ever was one. Not only is the paperwork a nightmare but the net is the same: *Story* and *Saunders*, two sides of the same make-believe coin.

When your name is Story, permission is granted to step into the darkness; to mine it for meaning.

We are our stories. True and otherwise.

Do I have a right to tell my story? The story of my family?

The only way to extinguish trouble's fire is to stop running.

To stop pretending.

To pay attention.

To tell hard truths.

To face consequences.

Over the years, I have cheated myself and others out of who I am; what I am capable of. I have been afraid at times to dream because I have been shown that acting on dreams comes at a cost. Instead, I've attempted to right the ship, seeking stability first and helping others pursue their dreams. Safety has its perks, but it has a way of leading one astray, too—of diminishing the very thing that sparks us alive. This is not the legacy I want to pass to my daughter and bonus son.

In kindergarten, we were asked to make a puppet of who we would be when we grew up. I made a bride. I was embarrassed when the other kids shared their firemen, doctors, and Supermans, but a bride was the only thing my five-year-old mind could picture. My only visual of the future was a symbol of wanting to be loved. I saw it in my mom and the other moms in my neighborhood as they kept house and tried to keep their minds from splintering from the tedium. I saw it in my dad and the other dads who worked so hard at their day jobs and the roles they thought they had to play. I see it now as my children look for acceptance from anyone other than themselves, a rite of passage. Although the feminist in me crinkles her forehead at that white dress and veil, my heart knows that it is in part my destiny: to love those who need it the most, including myself. In a world that is constantly twisting and turning in its evolution, casting people aside in obsolescence, this act of love comes in the form of telling our stories—of not letting the shapes and colors, rights and wrongs, fears and joys get smashed, halved, and then quartered into a junk pile, unaware of their original purpose.

When your name is Story, permission is granted; to bring light into the darkness and to course correct.

I write my story.

Because it is my name.

It is my birthright to tell you how I see it.

My name is Story.

Our name is Story.

Chapter 18
This is for the birds

"Don't take that!" he barks.

The waiter tries to keep his cool, but his eyes are wide, eyebrows raised into his hairline.

"It's for the birds." Dad brings it down a notch in tone, but the intensity is ever present. He reaches across the table, snatching the bread crusts from the plate with his calloused paws. He piles the discards into a napkin, pushes his way out the booth, and trudges to the front door of the restaurant. He's in a mood, so we all hold our breath until he is safely out the door without kicking it or muttering to a passerby. No broken glass; no innocents harmed. We can go. We find him tossing his crusts into the parking lot, softly encouraging a meal: "Here you go. No waste. Here you go." Crows eye him from above. I decide they are thankful and forgive the rudeness of this particular ritual, which happens at every meal, at any place—home or restaurant.

He has gone hungry. He knows the bellyache. If he can give, he does.

"This is for the birds," she murmurs.

I can see her so clearly from the early days at the junkyard. Mom sits at a desk surrounded by scraps of paper, official forms, and discarded sandwich crumbs. In front of her is the long yellow Formica counter hijacked from an old diner, with smelly old-timers hunkered down at every stool. Each one wants something. Grubby hands clutch greasy, unrecognizable hunks of metal. She is learning. A carburetor here, an alternator there, a brake drum, a rear differential. She writes it all down as if taking a lunch order, hoping to gather enough information. It's a desperate crowd today. No one is working on an old hobby car—a vintage Mustang or Bel Air they hope to pass down to a child or grandchild. No, this is the hard scrabble, the "I've got to move from point A to point B today, and I don't have much scratch to pay for this and I don't have time to deal with a woman who doesn't know anything about cars" crowd. They snarl. Mom didn't ask for this. This wasn't part of her plan. She heads out the back door, chest tight, looking for a shop lackey who can decipher the metal gibberish. Out of sight from the old-timers, Mom sighs violently. "This is for the birds."

She has known disappointment. How it simmers and reduces in the pan, leaving syrupy, concentrated fear mixed with resentment.

I look up. They are everywhere. Little hoppy birds, crows perched on power lines, and scrub jays heading to nests. Our elegant stand of Doug Firs is home to hundreds. The birds sweep down from the sky in between storms, gathering up worms, tiny insects, and pieces of this and that to take back to their cozy nests. They are my gauge for knowing when temperamental weather will roll in. I lean against my rusty old Ford truck, delighted by their weightlessness and ingenuity. How different they are from the bird lore featured in that old soap opera my mom loved so much. Those mythical Thornbirds led us astray. Winged small-screen legends pushing us to believe that beauty and meaning only come at great cost. As it turns out, thornbirds are real but they are not interested in impaling or singing themselves to death. Instead they are known for sculpting elaborate, thorny nests from sticks, twigs, and whatever else they can scavenge. They sing for practicalities—simply a form of communication rather than self-expression or sacrifice. Sometimes truth is far more interesting than myth. I tug a few leaves and twigs from under the windshield wiper blades of my old Ford, fling them to the ground, and wonder what kind of bird might swoop down and pick them up, use them for a nest.

Acknowledgments

When you've been writing and living a story as long as I have, you know that you exist less in a village and more in a bustling metropolis of support. Thank you to friends, family, and new friends alike who have contributed to this publishing effort. None of this would be possible without the outpouring of encouragement, financial support, and wisdom. In a time of mass silencing, especially of women's voices around the world, I feel especially honored that you chose this indie effort to champion.

A few special shout-outs:

Wheels:
- My first wheels to freedom: '83 Honda Civic.
- Salem Composite Descenders, who taught me courage.
- The Bike Peddler, who taught me to challenge the stories I thought I knew.
- My bikes, who challenged me and reinvented my body.

My first loves—Friendship:

- Colleen Drew Steving
- Ericka Laidemitt
- Eloise Thornberry Gonzalez

Champions:

- Kirk Delman
- Sarah Hillman
- Megan Richardson
- Jessica Amos
- Heather Wolfgang
- Laurel Goode
- Chantal Barton
- Brooke Schelar
- Bob and Kathy Saunders
- Cindi Stowell-Baczkowski

Earliest readers:

- Leslee Woodman
- Casimir Kopacki
- Ryan Reed
- Laurel Goode
- Berri Leslie
- Ellen Fagg Weist

Expertise:

- Michelle Kicherer, Founding Editor of Banana Pitch Press

- Literary Arts, Portland
- Luka Cohn (proofreader) and Gwendolyn Schulte at GRS Editorial (editing and design)
- Ryan Johnson—cover illustration

My foundation:

- Karen, Harry, Ryan

My everything:

- Dave, Peyton, Justin, Huck

A Note From the Editor

Banana Pitch Press is a nonprofit 501(c)3 indie press. Like all of our books to date, this book was made possible through donations. An amazing 76 individuals donated to make this book possible. Thank you, everyone! Special thanks to this book's Executive Editor, Jesse Bo Widmark, for his generous support and enthusiasm for all things car.

Our full list of donors is on our website, at BananaPitch.com.

Thank you and I hope you've enjoyed your trip to the junkyard.

Michelle Kicherer
Founding Editor
Banana Pitch Press

www.ingramcontent.com/pod-product-compliance
Lightning Source LLC
LaVergne TN
LVHW041936070526
838199LV00051BA/2805